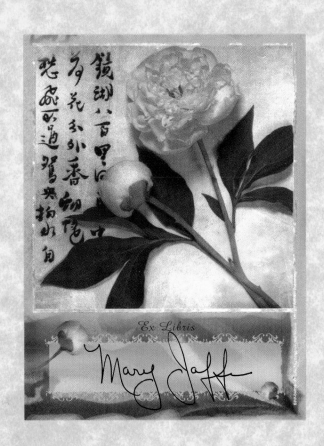

Ex Libris

Mary Jaffe

EVERY STEP A
LOTUS

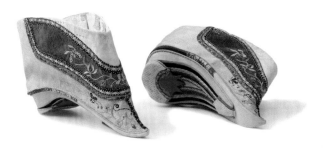

Once there was a doe who left imprints of the lotus blossom as she walked. She became the second wife of the Fanyu king and gave birth to a thousand-leaf lotus; on each leaf was a baby boy. Thus she received a thousand sons, who became the Thousand Buddhas of the Good Kalpa.

—"The Story of the Doe," *The Sutra on the Storehouse of Sundry Valuables*

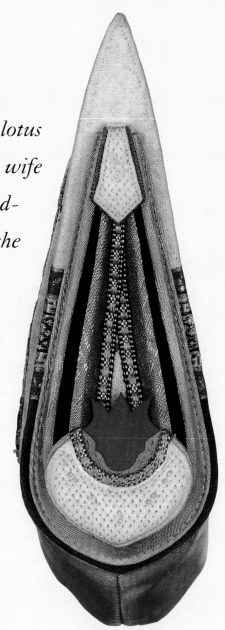

Every Step a
LOTUS
Shoes for Bound Feet

Dorothy Ko

THE BATA SHOE MUSEUM

UNIVERSITY OF CALIFORNIA PRESS
BERKELEY　　LOS ANGELES　　LONDON

University of California Press
Berkeley and Los Angeles, California

University of California Press, Ltd.
London, England

All inquiries about sale and distribution of this volume should be
directed to the University of California Press.

The Bata Shoe Museum Foundation
327 Bloor Street West
Toronto, Ontario M5S 1W7

LIBRARY OF CONGRESS CATALOGING-IN-PUBLICATION DATA

Ko, Dorothy, 1957–
    Every step a lotus : shoes for bound feet / Dorothy Ko.
      p. cm.
    "The Bata Shoe Museum."
    Includes bibliographical references and index.
    ISBN 0-520-23283-6 (cloth : alk. paper) — ISBN 0-520-23284-4
    (pbk. : alk. paper)
    1. Footbinding—China. 2. Shoes—China. I. Bata Shoe Museum
    Foundation. II. Title.

    GT498.F66 K6 2001
    391.4'1—dc21

                         2001027876

Printed and bound in Canada

10 09 08 07 06 05 04 03 02 01
10 9 8 7 6 5 4 3 2 1

The paper used in this publication meets the minimum requirements
of ANSI/NISO Z39.48-1992 (R 1997) (*Permanence of Paper*).

PAGE 1:
Northern-style shoes in lilac pink silk with blue silk vamp appliqué.
Length: 14 cm (5½ in.), 1890–1910. BSM P96.103.AB.

FRONTISPIECE:
Decorated sole of shoe with commercial ribbon in green and black.
Length: 14 cm (5½ in.), 1890–1910. BSM P96.103.A.

THIS PAGE:
Northern woman with the legs of her pants gathered inside leg
sashes and tight leggings. This style of dressing draws attention
to her lower leg, especially the bent ankle. Late Qing period.
Courtesy of Dr. Chi-sheng Ko.

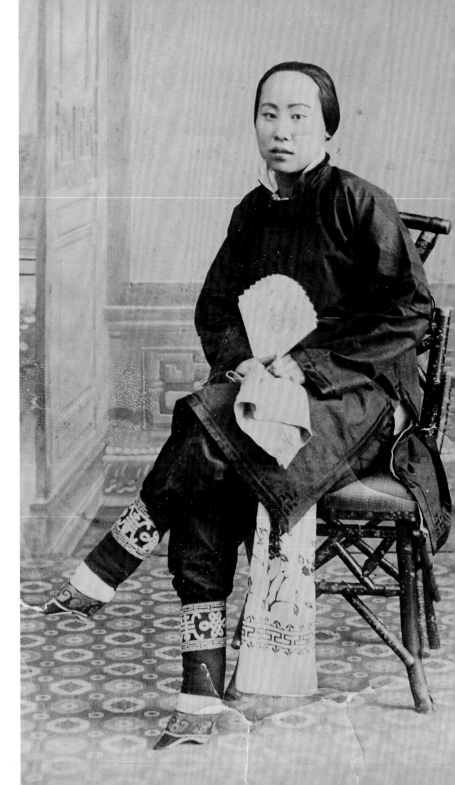

CONTENTS

Foreword   6

Acknowledgments   7

INTRODUCTION   9

1 ORIGINS   21

2 THE TIES THAT BIND   47

3 BODIES OF WORK   77

4 THE SPEAKING SHOE   97

5 A NEW WORLD   131

Notes   148

Bibliography   152

Photography Credits   155

Index   156

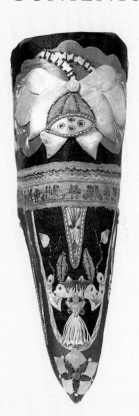

FOREWORD

All my life I have been fascinated by shoes, their history, and the reasons why such different shapes and decorative treatments evolved in different cultures. Shoes contribute to an understanding of cultures, life styles, and beliefs. They are also very personal, often disclosing details about the wearer's status in society, activities, and affiliations.

The study of Chinese lotus shoes—shoes for bound feet—is particularly intriguing since it opens up a whole new world. There is something mysterious and magical about these tiny shoes, which are often an item of exquisite beauty, full of symbolic designs and expressing the pride of women's artisanship.

As a child I saw my first lotus shoes in a museum in Europe and found them curious. In the 1950s, when visiting Singapore with my husband on family shoe business, I was surprised that shoes for bound feet were still being sold in the large Bata shoe store in Peninsula Plaza. Many years later I visited Glenn Roberts, a collector in New York, to view his magnificent collection. The richness and beauty of his lotus shoes were an eye-opener for me and gave me insight into a world that I was keen to know more about. The idea of researching this ancient custom and making the findings available to the public was born at that time.

Our foundation is fortunate that Dorothy Ko agreed to write this book and also curate an exhibition. Her woman's perspective on footbinding traditions and her personal enthusiasm were a great motivation for us all at The Bata Shoe Museum.

Every culture has its own way of celebrating beauty and expressing status. The lotus shoes of the Han women in China are a particularly fascinating story.

SONJA BATA, *Chairman, The Bata Shoe Museum Foundation*

ACKNOWLEDGMENTS

Most of the bodies are gone; only the shoes remain. This book could not have been written if not for the collectors of lotus shoes. Beverley Jackson once gave me a damaged shoe, urging me to take it apart and study its construction. It was an eye-opening lesson. Glenn Roberts generously shared his rich collection and ethnographic knowledge; although his shoes are not in this book, his impact certainly is. The same is true for Yang Shaorong. Dr. Chi-sheng Ko has been helpful in every way. The size of his unsurpassed collection is matched only by his expert knowledge and enthusiasm. The gracious support of Vincent V. Comer and Douglas D. L. Chong in lending artifacts and insights helped make this venture possible.

The support and vision of Mrs. Sonja Bata has made this project possible. At The Bata Shoe Museum, the dedication of the staff, especially Director Sharon McDonald and Curator Elizabeth Semmelhack, has made my involvement in this project as pleasant as it is edifying. The exhibition that inspired this book benefited from the good visual judgments of John Vollmer, Edmund Li, and Michael Peters. Sheila Levine at the University of California Press believes in my pair of footbinding books—this one on its material culture and the next one on its cultural history. These heroes and heroines who have contributed much behind the scenes deserve a public salute.

Jim Impoco urged me to write seriously about footbinding years ago. Although I finished writing this book before beginning my tenure at the Institute for Advanced Study, Princeton, during revision and preparation of illustrations I have benefited from the stimulating company of, among others, Benjamin Elman, Marilyn Aronberg Lavin, and Irving Lavin. Stacy Coons, K. C. Kelly, and Marcia Tucker are the most knowledgeable computer and library experts I have beseeched. Charlotte Furth, Susan Mann, Susan Naquin, and Bonnie Smith have each guided my study of embodiment and material culture. Chün-fang Yü has been as helpful as the Bodhisattva Guanyin she writes about. Besides these friends and colleagues, I am grateful to the Institute, Barnard College, the National Endowment for the Humanities, and the Guggenheim Foundation for the most precious gift of all: time to think about things.

Dorothy Ko

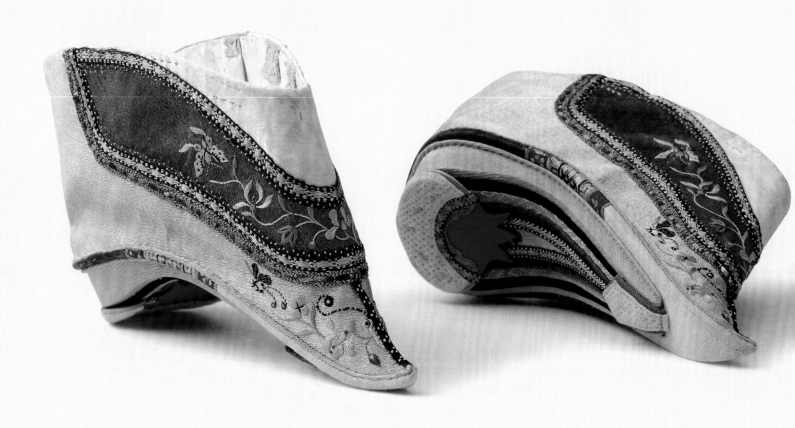

FIGURE 1
Northern-style shoes in lilac pink silk
with blue silk vamp appliqué.
Length: 14 cm (5½ in.), 1890–1910.
BSM P96.103.AB.

INTRODUCTION

ABOUT A DECADE AGO I woke up one morning to an article in the *Los Angeles Times* denouncing breast implants. Under the headline "Draw the Line at the Knife," it began with a rhetorical question: "If tiny feet suddenly became fashionable, would American women subject themselves to foot-binding?" As apt as the analogy may be, I found it odd that footbinding, a practice in a land five thousand miles away and that ended over half a century ago, still exercises such a grip on our imagination. In popular media, it remains synonymous with "women's oppression" worldwide. When a contributor to *Time* magazine lamented her relocation to London on a "dependent spouse visa," for instance, she quipped about her willingness to go along with the label: "Isn't that, after all, what all the progressive feminist education, those years of studying Virginia Woolf and the barbarism of Chinese foot-binding, was for?"[1]

THE POWER OF THE IMAGE

Since the image of footbinding remains so vivid long after its demise, it became clear to me that its symbolic power merits serious study, alongside its actual history. In fact, it is difficult to grasp what footbinding was really about without understanding its enormous power as an image. The practice has a contradictory hold on our imagination: it both fascinates and repels. It is a perfect target for feminist critique: photographs of crushed bones are so grotesque that they provoke a visceral reaction, and stories of women being reduced by pain to hobbling on their knees produce moral outrage.[2] Yet our reaction to footbinding is not entirely negative. In museum exhibits, we admire the intricate embroidery on the tiny shoes. Tender scenes in erotic novels and paintings of a man fondling his lover's foot can be pleasurable in their discreteness. And, on the fringes of mainstream culture, there are unabashed lovers of the bound foot. Foot fetishists have even invented a machine that bends the foot into an arch; they liken a woman with bound feet to a ballerina soaring on toes or a person wearing six-inch heels.[3] It would be hard to find a mass market for the foot-bending machine, but few would disagree that admiration for pretty feet runs deep in many cultures, including our own.

Not One Footbinding, but Many

Beyond the two extremes of condemnation and fantasy, there is a growing appetite for accurate empirical knowledge about Chinese footbinding. When I lecture on the subject in universities and museums, often before I even open my mouth someone would ask: "So when exactly did it start? Why did the Chinese women do it?" Powerful stereotypes aside, many aspects of the practice remain puzzling. Consider, for example, the range of outdoor footwear for women with bound feet—lacquered rain boots, overshoes with nail-pegged soles, or slip-on overshoes with soft padded heels. If footbinding was crippling and debilitating, as is often assumed, why would the women ever need such protective gear? Furthermore, if footbinding signaled a woman's leisure-class status, why are some of the soles caked with mud and dirt from the fields?

FIGURE 2, OPPOSITE
Southern-style overshoes with open toes, to protect lotus shoes from dirt in the garden or on the road.

Clockwise from top:
Overshoes in embroidered dark blue cotton with cotton heel. Tucked inside is a matching pair of shoes. Length: 9.5 cm (3¾ in.), 20th century. Collection of Douglas D. L. Chong.

Overshoes in embroidered silk upper and two-part cotton sole. Length: 11.3 cm (4½ in.), 19th century. Collection of Dr. Chi-sheng Ko.

Overshoes in dark blue appliquéd cotton and wooden sole reinforced with nail pegs. Length: 11.8 cm (4⅝ in.), 19th century. Collection of Dr. Chi-sheng Ko.

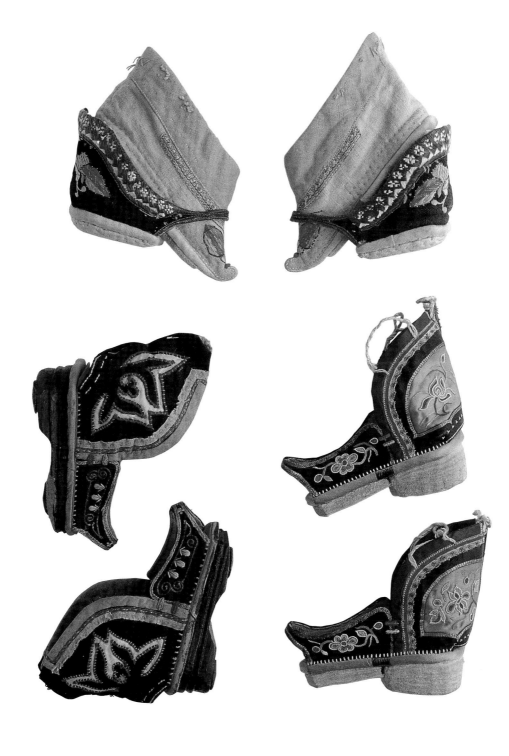

Shoes for bound feet can guide us to the material and bodily experiences of the women who made and wore them. I was therefore delighted when Sonja Bata, chairman of The Bata Shoe Museum Foundation, asked me to organize an exhibition entitled *Every Step a Lotus: Shoes in the Lives of Women in Late Imperial China*, which serves as the inspiration for this book. The premise of both the exhibition and this book is that footbinding was not a uniform practice—both the technique of binding and its meaning changed with time and place. Although there is not one cause for footbinding but many, it remained the single most important experience in a woman's life between the thirteenth and nineteenth centuries. It is thus helpful to adopt the women's perspectives and to understand their motives.

We should also bear in mind that throughout history, there were many women in China who did not bind their feet, due to ethnic and class barriers. It remained primarily an elite upper-class practice until the seventeenth and eighteenth centuries, when peasant daughters began to emulate it in growing numbers. In the nineteenth century, on the eve of its demise, footbinding grew so popular that it became the opposite of its former self—not exclusive but vulgar. It is therefore misleading to extrapolate from nineteenth-century missionary accounts the early history of the practice.

It is equally difficult to generalize about the ethnic background of women with bound feet. In the main, those who bound were restricted to Han Chinese, the majority ethnic group named after the Han dynasty (140 BCE–220 CE), a formative period during which the foundations of Chinese culture and Confucian government were laid. The masters of the last dynasty in China, the Qing (1644–1911), were an ethnic minority called the Manchus who repeatedly banned footbinding. Ironically, the policy contributed to the unprecedented popularity of the practice in the empire, spreading even to a handful of non-Han minority peoples on the southwestern borders. Yet exceptions abound even in the heyday of the practice. Women of the Hakka people,

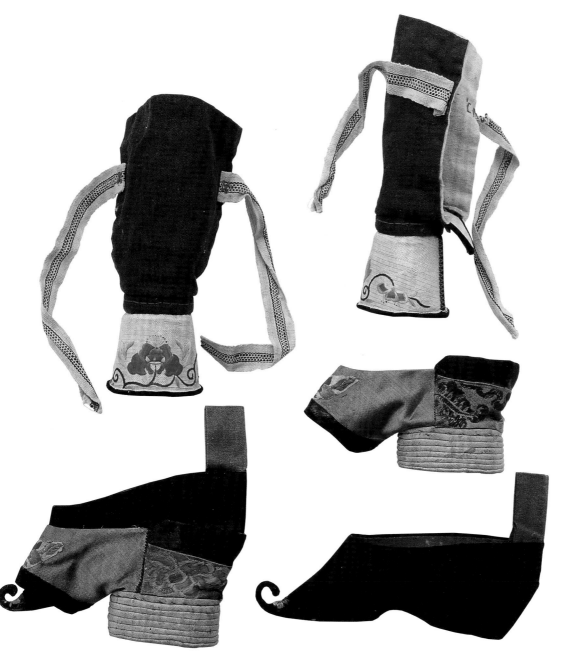

FIGURE 3

A woman with bound feet wore sleeping shoes to bed. Stepping out of bed, she might strap on a pair of heels or slip into soft-sided overshoes. Sometimes the heels were strapped onto feet covered only by the binding cloth, and then tucked inside boots.

Clockwise from top:
Cylindrical heels covered in pale blue silk with back flap of blue cotton. Width: 6.2 cm (2½ in.), 20th century. Collection of Dr. Chi-sheng Ko.

Soft-sided overshoes in blue silk with sturdy round heel made of layers of stitched cotton. Length: 12.7 cm (5 in.), 20th century. Collection of Dr. Chi-sheng Ko.

Socklike sleeping shoes with curled toe in blue cotton. Length: 18 cm (7⅛ in.), 20th century. Collection of Dr. Chi-sheng Ko.

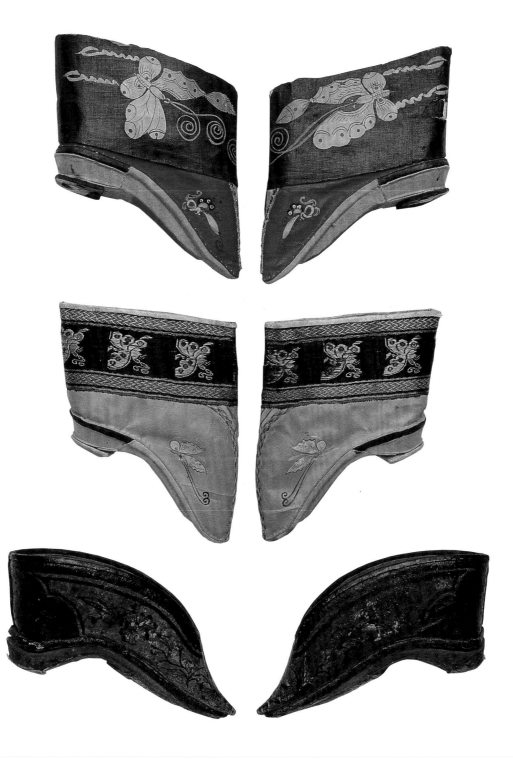

a unique group who were Han in ethnic origins but who developed non-Han customs, flaunted their famously large feet in the dry fields and battlefields.

NOT ONE EXPLANATION, BUT MANY

The purpose of this book is to present a new and more nuanced picture of footbinding by explaining its origin and spread before the nineteenth century in terms of women's culture and material culture. The usual explanations of "women were victims of beauty" or "men fetishized tiny feet" are not entirely wrong, but they oversimplify. Without denying the very real pain involved, I do not view footbinding as a senseless or perverted act. My goal is not to denounce but to explain by, so to speak, stepping into the women's shoes. We will see later in chapter 2 that footbinding was an entirely reasonable course of action for a woman who lived in a Confucian culture that placed the highest moral value on domesticity, motherhood, and handwork. The ideal Confucian woman was one who worked diligently with her hands and body, and those who did so were amply rewarded in terms of power in the family, communal respect, and even imperial recognition. The binding of feet created a woman who fit these ideals.

Yet such is the contradictory nature of footbinding that it can be a profoundly anti-Confucian and amoral undertaking. Maiming one's own body, the progeny of parents, is anti-filial, as is often charged in the modern anti-footbinding literature. Furthermore, when practiced by the "wrong" women— prostitutes and other temptresses—footbinding could distract the good son and husband from his Confucian duties, leading to the downfall of the family. This double-faced image of footbinding stems from the conflicting nature of demands placed on the Chinese woman, who could be either the saintly mother or the temptress, but not both. In this book I will focus on the former group, women lucky enough to be born into respectable households and groomed by their mothers to be good wives and mothers.

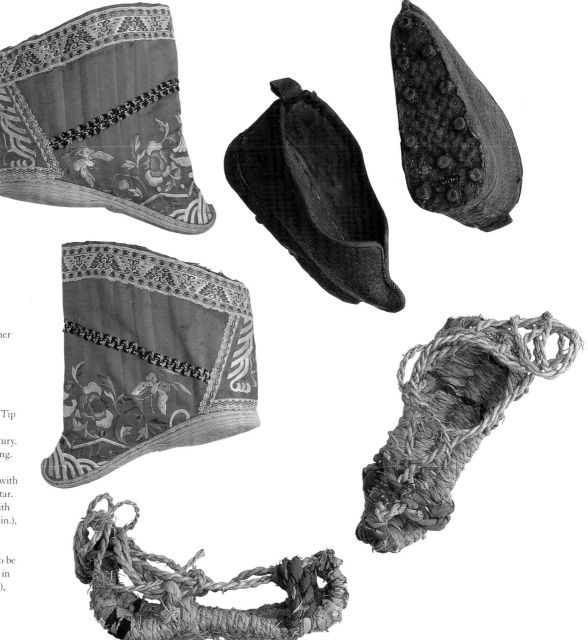

FIGURE 5
Extra protection from foul weather
or rugged terrain.

Clockwise from left:
Padded overboots in orange silk
with cotton sole. Top and vamp
edged with commercial ribbons. Tip
decorated with wave patterns.
Length: 19 cm (7½ in.), 20th century.
Collection of Douglas D. L. Chong.

Snow shoes made of felt treated with
an unknown substance, possibly tar.
Layered fabric sole reinforced with
metal pegs. Length: 18.5 cm (7¼ in.),
20th century. BSM P01.33.AB.

Straw sandals with curled toes, to be
strapped onto shoes for trekking in
the hills. Length: 20.1 cm (7⅞ in.),
20th century. BSM P01.29.AB.

Once footbinding became an established custom, the patina of "tradition" alone became a strong enough motivation for mothers to pass it on. Over time, a rich array of rituals evolved around the binding of feet and the exchange of shoes among relatives and friends. These rituals—concealed from men in the women's rooms—celebrated the women's skills and became a focal point of female identity. Simply put, my thesis is that the binding of feet is similar to the making of shoes in one important aspect: both display a woman's efforts and pride; they are testimonies to a woman's status in a society that valued domesticity and women's handwork. When these values came to be attacked as "feudal" at the dawn of the modern age, around the same time when daughters of the lower classes vied to imitate the practice, footbinding went into irrevocable decline.

SHOES AS TEXTS

My conclusions are based on a careful study of evidence ranging from archaeological findings to shoes in the collections of the Bata Shoe Museum and private collectors.[4] The Chinese used a variety of names to refer to shoes for bound feet—including arched shoes (*gongxie*), embroidered slippers (*xiuxie*), and gilded lilies (*jinlian*, which also refers to the bound feet in particular and to the customs associated with footbinding in general). In this book we adopt a modern English term, lotus shoes.

As a historian whose métier is the written word, I have learned to treat material objects as informative sources despite the difficulties involved in dating, classification, and interpretation. Compounding the difficulty in reconstructing the historical meaning of footbinding is the fact that the majority of the lotus shoes extant today are dated no earlier than the nineteenth century, the very period when the practice had begun to decline. It is understandable that until foreign travelers and missionaries became fascinated by the practice and collected shoes as exotic souvenirs, few in China had bothered to save these mundane objects. Unfortunately, the same modern bias is true for the bulk of the textual record documenting footbinding, most of which has been written since the late eighteenth century.

My method is to "read" the artifacts against whatever relevant textual evidence I can find to make them "talk to" one another. Particularly revealing are verse and prose written by women, which open our eyes to their lives in the inner chambers of a Chinese house and showcase the symbolic and economic importance of embroidery, shoe-making, and textile work to the women and their families. Without returning women to the center of Chinese domestic life, our understanding of footbinding would be incomplete. The most authoritative study of footbinding to date, Howard Levy's *Chinese Footbinding: The History of a Curious Erotic Custom*, falls short despite its encyclopedic treatment of the subject because the author failed to take the women's material culture and domestic environment seriously.

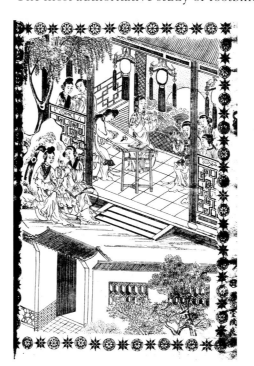

FIGURE 6
Woodblock print from a shoe-pattern book, showing women making shoes. Right margin inscription: "Moruntang gailiangban" (Revised edition issued by the Lustrous Ink Studio). Left margin inscription: "April, second year of the republic" (1913). BSM P01.32.

In the pages that follow I have reconstructed a picture of women with bound feet living and working in their domestic contexts in the eighteenth century, at the height of the Qing dynasty. After discussing the origins of footbinding and a woman's place in the house, I focus on the material aspects of footbinding and shoe-making: the tools needed, the procedures, the wealth of symbolism on the shoes, and the

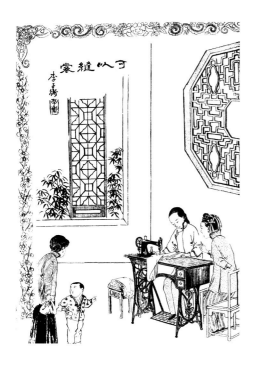

amazing regional variations in style. The story of the eventual demise of footbinding as a social practice in the second half of the nineteenth and early twentieth centuries is well-documented in Chinese and English scholarship.[5] So, too, is the story of the exotic and erotic enticements of small feet, which has long captivated the reading public.[6] Given this history of selective reporting, it may sound odd when I contend that in eighteenth-century China, footbinding had less to do with the exotic or the sublime than with the mundane business of having to live in a woman's body in a man's world.

FIGURE 7
Old values, new tools. Woodblock print from shoe-pattern book showing women working with the modern sewing machine. Right margin inscription: "Moruntang gailiangban" (Revised edition issued by the Lustrous Ink Studio). Left margin inscription: "April, second year of the republic" (1913). BSM P01.32.

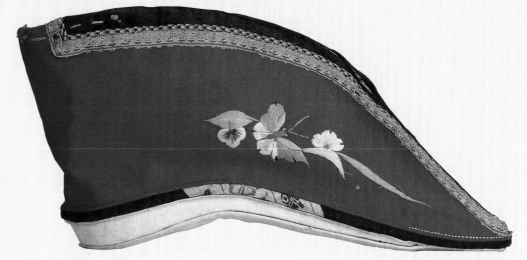

FIGURE 8, RIGHT
Northern-style shoe in red silk with
gently arched wooden sole covered
in white cotton. Length: 17.2 cm
(6¾ in.), 20th century. BSM s99.31.

FIGURE 9, BELOW
Shoe in pink silk with arched wedge
heel covered in blue silk. Length:
11.5 cm (4½ in.), 20th century.
BSM s84.163A.

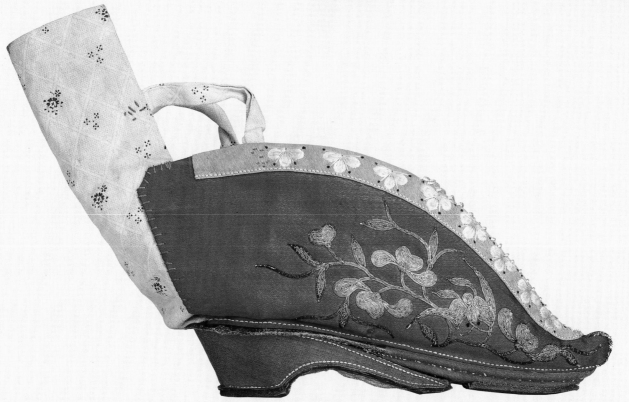

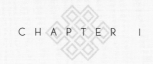

CHAPTER I

ORIGINS

IN 1975 A TEAM of Chinese archaeologists discovered a treasure trove when they unearthed the tomb of Huang Sheng, wife of a distant imperial clansman, in the southern city of Fuzhou, Fujian province. There, the body of Lady Huang (1227–43) was found in her coffin, her feet wrapped in strips of gauze cloth and tagged inside a pair of tiny shoes. Packed in a pouch, among the 354 pieces of textile preserved in the couple's wardrobe for the underworld, were five other pairs of her shoes. Their sizes range from 13.3 to 14 cm in length and 4.5 to 5 cm in width (5¼–5½ by 1¾–2 in.), which is comparable to the average of those found in museum collections today. The existence of other everyday items in the tomb—including socks and a holder for sanitary napkins stained with blood—leaves little doubt that all the shoes were intended for actual wear instead of ceremonial purposes.[1] For those in search of the origins of footbinding, Huang Sheng's tomb was the Holy Grail. Since the young bride hailed from a high-ranking official family, we can now say with certainty that by the early thirteenth century,

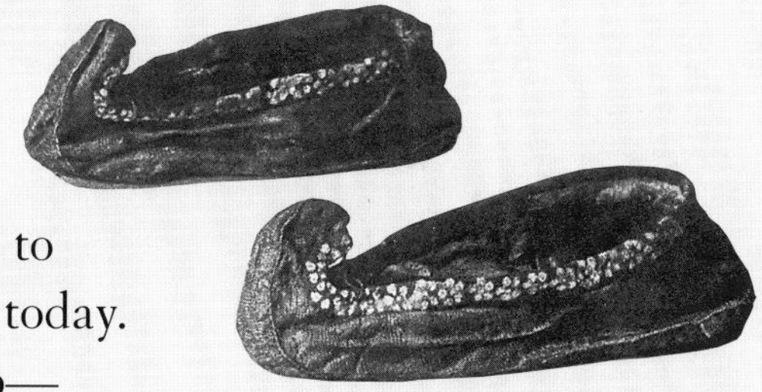

FIGURE 10
Shoes from the tomb of Lady Huang Sheng. Brown silk *luo*-tabby upper with hemp sole. Topline edged with printed gold plum-blossom motif. Silk ribbon tied into a bow sewn to tip of shoes. Length: 14 cm (5½ in.), 13th century. From *Chinese Costumes*, p. 305, pl. 244. Courtesy of the Fujian Province Museum.

footbinding was practiced by the daughters and wives of high officials in the southern coastal city.

Yet the question of origins cannot be laid to rest so easily. As informative as Lady Huang's wardrobe is, it opens up new and larger questions that she alone could not answer. Was she among the first to bind? How widespread was the practice in her times? What was her motivation? Her shoes are even more puzzling: all six pairs are, like the pair pictured here, made of soft silk tabby (*luo*) sewn onto a flat sole of coarse hemp. The edges are decorated with silk ribbons from toe to heel. All feature a sharp upturned toe that differs substantially in style and construction from shoes worn in the eighteenth and nineteenth centuries. Many of the modern regional styles have stiff wooden soles and high heels to provide support, and feature toes that point downward. One can imagine that the wearers of these two types of shoes walked with a different gait, with the body weight distributed differently. Was Lady Huang's footbinding the same as the footbinding we know? To answer these questions fully we need to first explore origins before we survey more archaeological and textual evidence.

When confronted with something unfamiliar, one of our first instincts is to ask, how did it come about? Knowing the history of an alien object or concept—from beginning to end—helps us master it by putting it into our frame of understanding. But the question of origins is always easier to ask than to answer. Take for instance the birth of movies. While it can be said that Thomas Edison invented the motion picture when he showed, in the Chicago World's Fair of 1893, a sequence of moving pictures in a special cabinet called a Kinetoscope, almost two decades before then a photographer named Eadweard Muybridge had used still cameras to capture the full gallop of a horse on a racetrack. Furthermore, movies would not have been made and marketed if not for the development of the Hollywood studio system in the early decades of the twentieth century. Without the gathering of talent and money in sunny southern California, the technical "hardware" would have sat idle, or been put to different uses. To go even further, this coming together of technological and human factors was far from fortuitous but was propelled by fundamental shifts in visual culture and popular entertainment.

The beginnings of cultural phenomena as complex as the movie industry or footbinding can seldom be located in a single point in time. Nor is it simply a matter of finding one definitive piece of empirical evidence. The search for the origins of footbinding is not entirely an objective exercise, a matter of lining up all the available evidence. In the process of interpreting the evidence, sooner or later we would have to define the essence of footbinding, which involves a degree of subjective judgment. Is it the hardware, shoes with pointy toes, or the software, a preference for tiny feet, that signifies footbinding? What do we make of the fact that Lady Huang's shoes, although small, do not at all look like shoes for bound feet as we know them?

MATERIAL EVIDENCE FROM THE TOMBS

Scattered evidence from thirteenth-century tombs suggests that Lady Huang's style of a prominent upturned toe could well be the norm for women in the Southern Song dynasty (1127–1279). Not long after the discovery of the lady's bountiful wardrobe, a pair of shoes similar in style to hers but made of welded silver plates turned up in a tomb in Quzhou, a city in the province of Zhejiang about 300 kilometers (186 miles) north of Fuzhou. Buried in the tomb were a scholar, Shi Shengzu, who died in 1274, and his second wife. The pair of silver shoes was a memento of Shi's first wife, who passed away in 1240, around the same time as Lady Huang. Her name, Luo Shuangshuang, was inscribed on the sole. The shoes, funerary objects made especially for burial, are as small as Lady Huang's, measuring 14 cm long and 4.5 cm wide

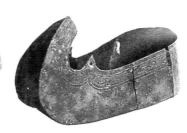

FIGURE 11
Silver shoes with dramatic upturned toes from the tomb of Shi Shengzu. The name of his first wife, Luo Shuangshuang, is etched on the sole. Length: 14 cm (5½ in.), 13th century. From Gao Hongxing, *Chanzu shi*, no page. Courtesy of Shanghai Literature and Art Publishing House.

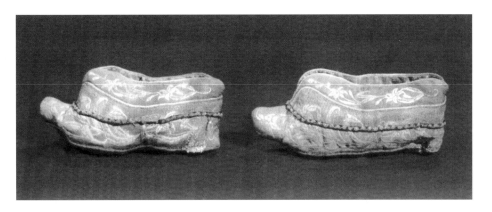

FIGURE 12
Imperial footwear. Shoes of a queen of Jin (1115–1234), a kingdom in present-day Manchuria established by the Jurchens, an ethnic minority people who were the ancestors of the Manchus. Embroidered upper made of green *luo*-gauze with camel-colored band, sole made of hemp. These shoes were not for bound feet, but the upturned toes resemble those from thirteenth-century Song tombs. Length: 23 cm (9 in.), 12th to 13th centuries. From Zhu Qixin, "Royal Costumes of the Jin Dynasty," p. 110. Reprinted with the permission of Heilongjiang Province Cultural and Archeological Relics Institute.

(5½ by 1¾ in.).[2] Taken together, the shoes of these two ladies provide strong evidence for the existence of a style with exaggerated upturned toes popular in the southern cities.

Several years later, in the town of De'an in the neighboring province of Jiangxi, archaeologists unearthed another tomb that yields collaborative evidence. Researchers found the body of a Madame Zhou (1240–74), daughter and wife of officials, who was buried with seven pairs of shoes. Decorated with a butterfly knot on the vamp, the shoes have toes that curve upward, albeit less prominently than the ones we have seen. These shoes are longer (18–22 cm; 7–8⅝ in.) and wider (5–6 cm; 2–2⅜ in.)—large enough for unbound feet. A published photograph of the young woman's well-preserved body shows that her big toe was bent upwards, conforming to the shape of her shoes.[3]

The tombs of these three thirteenth-century ladies suggest that daughters and wives in Southern Song official families wrapped their feet with cloth to alter their shape, and that the prevalent style, with an upward-bending big toe, was the opposite of the norm in subsequent centuries. Despite the difference in style, if we define "footbinding" as wrapping the foot with a strip of cloth to make it smaller and narrower, then we would have to conclude that a version of it was practiced in the thirteenth century. The evidence from the tombs, however, does not tell us why small feet came to be favored in the first place. What cultural forces were powerful enough to compel these young ladies to change their body and appearance?

THE CHINESE CINDERELLA

The most important factor in the development of footbinding was the growth of a Cinderella complex from the ninth to thirteenth centuries. Versions of the Cinderella story can be found throughout the world, but among its earliest appearances is in a ninth-century collection of Chinese stories. This collection contains a wealth of tales of ghosts, animals, plants, and fantastic events from the Tang dynasty (618–907), a cosmopolitan empire reaching as far as Central Asia. The storyteller presented the tale of the Chinese Cinderella—her name is Yexian—as part of an oral tradition from an area dotted with streams and grottoes in the south (see "Yexian, the Chinese Cinderella").

The story bears a striking resemblance to the German fable told by the Grimm brothers one millennium later. With the exceptions of the sister's mutilated toe and the fairy godmother, all the main elements of the plot are present: the jealous stepmother, the animal medium, the grand ball, and the lost shoe. In Europe, the fairytale lends itself to psychoanalytic interpretations that relate shoes to castration anxieties. The Chinese story reveals a somewhat different set of attitudes toward shoes and sexuality. A focus on them may shed light on the cultural forces that brought footbinding into being.

We notice, for instance, that the fish and the slipper were described in almost identical terms: the exact measurements of both were given in feet and inches; the size of the fish grows from puny to gigantic, whereas the slipper, already small, seems to shrink even further. This fixation on size and measurement is a key device that established the beauty of the bound foot in the lyrical tradition, described below. In many folk songs from a later period, too, big-footed daughters complain, in language similar to that about the miraculous carp, that their feet keep growing no matter how tightly they bind them. In this context it is hard to resist reading the fish as a sublimated foot. In ancient China, both the fish and the foot were related to fecundity: the fish was a fertility symbol found on Neolithic pottery, and legend has it that the

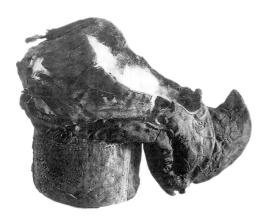

FIGURE 13
Imperial footwear. Shoes from the tomb of the Ming emperor Wanli (r. 1573–1620). Pale red silk upper with embroidered lotus, pine, and bamboo motifs. The upturned toe resembles that of thirteenth-century shoes, whereas the cylindrical heel represents a new development. Length: 12 cm (4¾ in.); height of cylindrical heel: 4.5 cm (1¾ in.), early 17th century. From Wang Yan, *Wanli dihou de yichu*, p. 112. Reprinted with the permission of Dingling Museum.

YEXIAN, THE CHINESE CINDERELLA

According to an oral tradition among people in the south, in the time before the first imperial dynasty, Qin (221–206 BCE), there lived a chieftain cave master named Wu whom the locals called Wu-the-Cave. His first wife, the mother of his daughter Yexian, died and he remarried. The young Yexian was wise, a darling of her father who loved her abilities in panning (or "fishing") for gold. After he died, the stepmother sent Yexian into the steep hills to gather firewood and into the deep river to fetch water. One day she found a carp with golden eyes and red barbels and kept it in a basin. Barely over two inches at the time, the carp grew day after day and outgrew basin after basin. Finally it could not fit into any vessel, so Yexian moved it to a pond behind the house, sharing whatever food she had left. Whenever she approached, the carp would emerge and rest its head on the edge; when others appeared it would dive back into the water.

Seeing this, the stepmother tricked the daughter and said, "Look how hard you've been working! I've got you a new overcoat." Making Yexian shed her old coat, the mother sent her to fetch water from a faraway stream. Slowly she wrapped herself in her stepdaughter's coat and, hiding a sharp knife in the sleeve, walked toward the pond and called out to the carp. The fish raised its head from the water and was killed instantly. She cooked the large fish for dinner—it had grown over ten feet long—and relished the extraordinary taste of its meat. The bones she hid under the cesspit.

Yexian, days later realizing that the carp was no longer in the pond, went to the fields and wailed. Sud-denly a person with wild hair and plain clothes came down from the sky to counsel her: "Don't cry. Your stepmother has killed the fish, but its bones are in the cesspit. Go and hide them in your room and whatever you want, ask and you shall receive." Henceforth the daughter enjoyed all the gold, pearls, garments, and food she desired.

On the day of the Cave Festival, the stepmother left Yexian behind to watch the garden. The daughter, waiting long enough to see that the stepmother was far away, went out wearing a jade-green silk coat and golden slippers. The stepmother's own daughter, recognizing Yexian at the party, said, "Doesn't she look like my elder sister?" and the stepmother grew suspicious. Yexian hurried away but dropped one slipper, which local people picked up. When the stepmother returned home, she found Yexian sleeping in the garden with her arms around a tree, and she did not think twice about the incident.

Neighboring the Land of Caves was an island in the sea, the seat of a mighty kingdom called Tuohan, which controlled scores of islands stretching thousands of miles. The Cave people sold the slipper to the Tuohan king, who ordered his attendants to try it on. But the slipper was smaller by an inch than even the smallest foot. He then ordered all the women in his kingdom to do the same, but the slipper fit no one. The shoe was light as a feather and did not crumple when it hit a pebble or stone. The Tuohan king, suspecting foul play, threw the Cave people into prison and tried to torture a confession from them, but no one knew where it came

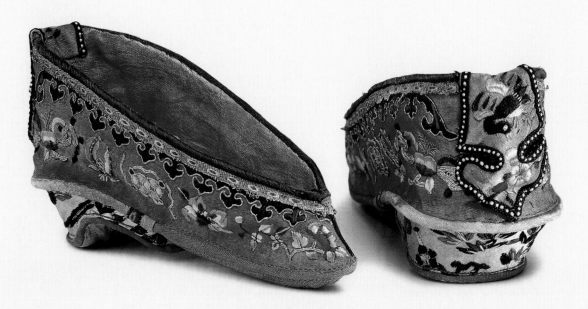

Tiny silk slippers embroidered in multicolor silk floss and gold metal thread.
Length: 11 cm (4⅜ in.), 20th century. BSM P88.221.AB.

from. They told the king the slipper was found by the roadside, and that they inquired at all the nearby households but to no avail. The king, becoming curious, went to inspect Wu-the-Cave's house and found Yexian. When he had her try on the slipper, he knew she was the one. She appeared in her jade-green coat, walking with hesitant steps in the slippers and looking as radiant as a beauty from the sky. The king returned to his kingdom with Yexian, taking the fish bones with them.

The stepmother and her daughter were felled by flying rocks and died. The Cave people, mourning them, buried their remains in a stone trough and named it the "Tomb of Regretful Daughters." The people made offerings to the spirits so that they would grant descendants. All Cave people wishing for a girl would have their prayers answered. The Tuohan king made Yexian his exalted queen, and for a year he greedily beseeched the fish bones for boundless treasures and jewels. But the next year the responses stopped. The king buried the bones by the shore, covering them with a thousand bushels of pearls and marking the boundaries with gold. Later when his troops mutinied, the generals used the loot to pay their soldiers. The site was erased by the ocean waves.

—From Duan Chengshi, *Youyang zazu* (Miscellanies from Youyang)

mother of Houyi, a cultural hero, became pregnant after stepping on a footprint. The prominence of the carp in the plot of the Yexian tale suggests that these ancient folkways about the connection between the foot and sexuality had resonance in the ninth century.

The Chinese storyteller's intended moral about girls is equally revealing. We do not know if Yexian lived happily ever after; she disappeared from the story after her marriage to the king. Nevertheless, the death of the stepmother redressed the scales. The transformation of the stepmother's tomb into a shrine for the spirits who grant daughters was a reversal of familiar social practice. We know that the Chinese prayed for boys, not girls, to continue the family line. Could it be that the storyteller was suggesting that a girl with the smallest feet in the empire was valuable, despite prevalent prejudice? In other words, isn't it entirely reasonable to think of footbinding as a way to enhance the value of girls, an attempt to reverse or at least remedy the societal preference for boys?

It is difficult to tell the extent to which the Yexian story reflects actual social practices in ninth-century China. It is even harder to map the geography in the story onto the real world. The storyteller stated he heard it from a retainer who hailed from the land of caves in Yongzhou, a certifiable district in the province of Guangxi, on the southwestern frontiers of the empire. But similar claims of certitude abound in the genre of fantastic tales. The southwestern landscape is indeed dotted with streams and grottoes, but so is the magical homeland of immortals in Daoist and folk religions. We should think of the Southland—the birthplace of Cinderellas—as a literary place that corresponds only dimly to actual geography. Indeed, a large body of romantic poetry since the fifth and sixth centuries had firmly etched in the Chinese reader's mind a picture of an imaginary Southland populated by willful kings frolicking in the rear palace gardens with willowy harem dancers. More than the Yexian story, it was these popular poems that cemented the association between small feet and princely romance.

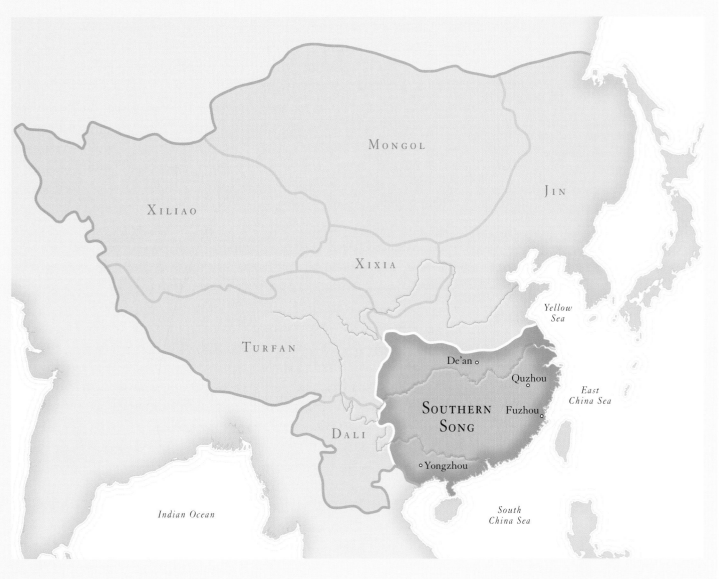

CHINA UNDER THE SOUTHERN SONG DYNASTY, CA. 1208

MONGOL

JIN

XILIAO

XIXIA

TURFAN

Yellow
Sea

De'an

Quzhou

SOUTHERN
SONG

Fuzhou

East
China Sea

DALI

Yongzhou

Indian Ocean

South
China Sea

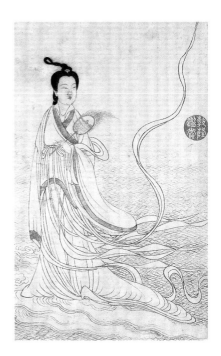

FIGURE 14
Goddess of the River Luo. The nymph in Cao Zijian's poem was said to be wearing "distant roaming slippers," about which little is known. In this painting inspired by the poem "Rhapsody on the Luo River Goddess," the painter hinted at a style of footwear with prominent triangular upturned toes. Wei Jiu-ding, Yuan dynasty, fl. 1352, hanging scroll, monochrome ink on paper. From National Palace Museum, *Glimpses into the Hidden Quarters*, p. 31, pl. 16-2. Courtesy of National Palace Museum, Taipei, Taiwan, Republic of China.

VERSES OF THE FRAGRANT TOILETTE

The Yexian story was but a part of a long literary tradition whereby poets and storytellers fixated on parts of a maiden's body as a stand-in for the beauty or worth of her entire person. One of the earliest of these maidens to receive lyrical attention is the Goddess of the River Luo, a nymph who embodies the female *yin* essence. In his seminal tribute to the goddess, third-century poet Cao Zijian wrote of her ephemeral allure as she appears to her lover the shaman-king (and vicariously the reader) on a distant bank below the cliffs:

> *She is dimly descried like the moon obscured by light clouds,*
> *She drifts airily like whirling snow in streaming wind.*
> *Gaze at her from afar,*
> *And she glistens like the sun rising over morning mists,*
> *Examine her close up,*
> *And she is dazzling as lotus emerging from limpid ripples…*
> *She drapes herself in the shimmering glitter of a gossamer gown,*
> *Wears in her ears ornate gems of carnelian and jade,*
> *Bedecks her hair with head ornaments of gold and halcyon plumes,*
> *Adorns herself with shining pearls that illuminate her body.*
> *She treads in patterned Distant Roaming slippers,*
> *Trails a light skirt of misty gauze.*
> *Obscured by the fragrant lushness of thoroughwort,*
> *She paces hesitantly in a mountain nook.*[4]

So popular was this poem that it inspired numerous other poems and paintings. In due time, the fluttering ribbons and sleeves on the goddess's dress and the silk slippers that guided her tread across water became metaphors for feminine beauty in general and her sexual appeal in particular. Her garments were enticing because they indicated the movement of the goddess's concealed body. The shaman-king's lingering gaze in the poem lent an erotic charge to ribbons and slippers—exterior clothing, not the body itself—that would come to define the appeal of footbinding in a later age. There was no emphasis at this point, however, on the size of the goddess's feet.

Poetic attention on the goddess's feet became more lavish and explicit as time went on, and in the waning years of the Tang dynasty, the golden age of Chinese poetry, a new lyric genre developed that carried the literary interest in female feet and footwear to new heights. Often called the Fragrant Toilette, this type of lyric scrutinizes the female body—set against the props of ornate garments and furniture—with unabashed eyes, resulting in a highly sensuous picture of the boudoir. The laureate of this genre is Han Wo (844–ca. 923), a scholar of the Tang imperial academy whose erudition earned him privileged access to the inner court. Instead of losing sleep over the political and military crises that were to bring down the mighty dynasty in 907, Han and his friends wrote fondly of the parting of bed curtains, trembling hairpins, and the red underwear of a disrobing lover. Although not among his most famous or polished work, "Ode to the Slippers" captures one small aspect of the fin-de-siècle splendor:

> Glowing, glowing, six inches of succulent flesh;
> Embroidered slipper in white silk, lined in red.
> Not much of a romantic, the southern dynasty emperor,
> Yet he prefers the golden lotus to green leaves.[5]

Unlike the distant picture of the river nymph in the earlier poem, these lines have a visceral appeal. The first two lines assault the senses of the reader with two sets of contrast: that between the lustrous flesh of the foot and the tactile stitches on the shoes, and that between the white outside and red inside of the shoe itself. The blatant mention of six inches of flesh in the first line set off a philological debate centuries later: is it proof that footbinding existed in the tenth century? How small is six inches? It seems to me wise not to be so literal minded. What is more important is that this poem establishes the two aesthetic ideals associated with footbinding in the subsequent centuries: the lure of exact measurements, which echoes the presentation of the carp and gold slipper in the Yexian story, as well as the contrast between the bare skin of the foot and the ornamentation of the shoe. This tension between flesh and dress is a sure formula for sensuous appeal.

The last two lines of "Ode to the Slippers" introduce two salient motifs of the origin myths of footbinding that came to flourish in the thirteenth and fourteenth centuries—a decadent ruler and a lotus blossom. The "southern dynasty emperor" is Xiao Baojian, also known as the Duke of Donghun, who ruled the southern kingdom of Qi from 499 to 501. He was said to have shaped gold leaves into lotus blossoms on the floor and had his favorite consort, Pan, tread on them. The enraptured duke exclaimed: "Every step a lotus," twisting a Buddhist reference to the path of piety into an anti-Buddhist statement of wanton lust (hence the poet's indictment of his lack of a refined sense of romance in the third line.)[6] One year after the duke's death, his kingdom collapsed, and Consort Pan became a classic femme fatale in the history books. Centuries later, storytellers expounded on the lotus imagery, by then firmly identified with the bound foot, and made her into the first woman to bind her feet.

It is difficult to tell if Han Wo thought so. Chinese poetry is often deliberately ambiguous, offering the joy of multiple interpretations. The last line of the ode, in which he contrasted "golden lotus" to "green leaf" (literally "teeth"), functions primarily as a contrast in colors for dramatic effect, in harmony with the second line. But a bolder reading is possible, since the word "teeth" can also mean the stilts of a clog, or a heel lift of a shoe. So we may

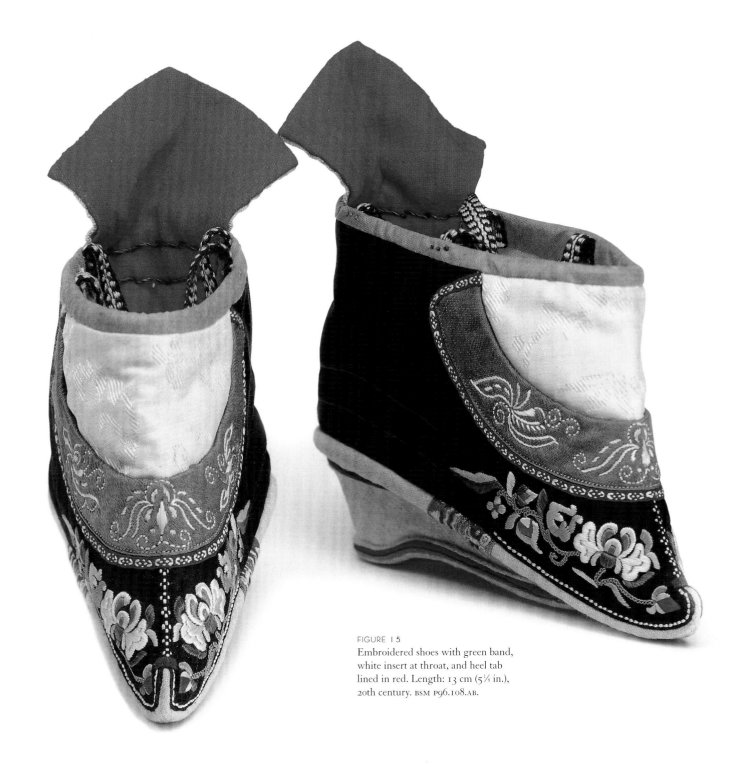

FIGURE 15
Embroidered shoes with green band,
white insert at throat, and heel tab
lined in red. Length: 13 cm (5⅛ in.),
20th century. BSM P96.108.AB.

read this line as a statement on the poet's aesthetics of footwear: discreet accessories—a green heel lift or tab—can enhance the main attraction, the lotus shoe. Indeed, this kind of delicate artistic balance is exactly what makes shoes for bound feet so beautiful.

It would be wrong to insist that this ode is proof for the Tang origins of footbinding. Neither is there any indication that the historic Consort Pan, or any fifth-century woman, wrapped her feet with strips of fabric. But the consort can be said to have prefigured the connection between the lotus, dancing, and sensuality in the Southland, which later constituted footbinding's main appeal. She was well known enough to the readers of "Ode to the Slippers" that the poet did not have to name her explicitly. With the retelling of her story, the association between an erotic gaze on female feet and lotus imagery was sealed in the minds of tenth-century readers.

The eroticism of feet and shoes was further developed in a famous anthology of boudoir poetry that appeared in the 940s, shortly after Han Wo's death. Aptly entitled *Among the Flowers*—flowers allude to feminine beauty and sensuality—the large collection of song-lyrics was set to music and performed in banquets in court and society. Among the numerous odes to objects in the boudoir is "Rhapsody of the Brocade Shoe" by Wen Tingyun (812–ca. 870), a founder of the song lyrics genre. Consider two lines from this long poem: "Brightly the Weaving Maid ties her feet; Lovingly the Moon Goddess knots the cocoon filaments." The expression "ties her feet" is ambiguous and can be read "tidying up her feet." But clearly the poet's attention on the Weaving Maid's feet, used to peddle the spindle-wheel or the foot loom, is mildly erotic. So, too, is his choice of the word "knots," which evokes marital intimacy by alluding to "tying the wedding knot." In ancient legends, the Weaving Maid and Moon Goddess were associated with the sanctity of textile work—industry being the foremost female virtue—and here the poet imparted a romantic if not an erotic gloss to the mundane work of spinning, weaving, and shoe-making.

The song-lyrics in *Among the Flowers* indicate that the poetic attention on footwear heralded in the Fragrant Toilette genre had become a fixture in the Chinese lyrical tradition. It is clear that by the tenth century, a literary image of footbinding was in full bloom in verse and storytelling. In themselves these texts did not "prove" footbinding's existence as a social practice, but they promoted a set of cultural values—a Cinderella complex if we may—that made the practice appear reasonable if not downright desirable in some quarters in the waning years of the Tang dynasty. The ancient association of the foot with fecundity received a shot of erotic charge when slippers became the focus of attention. The medieval river nymph, also linked to fecundity, reappeared as the consort of earthly kings and dukes—the goddess of unbridled desire. The Cinderella complex signals a shifting emphasis from sex-for-procreation to sex-for-pleasure, the most basic impulse that gave birth to footbinding as a literary image and a social practice.

Dance, Dance, Dance

Footbinding became an actual bodily practice when men and women sought to act out the poetic images, in jest and with trepidation at first but in a more physical and serious way as time went on. We know close to nothing about how the process happened or its psychological effects, but clearly it is rooted in larger shifts in cultural tastes and involves more than one instigator or location. In all likelihood, this practice began slowly in the eleventh century after the fall of the Tang, most probably first among entertainers and professional dancers, and then spread when respectable housewives chose to adopt the fashion and styles of entertainers. In other words, footbinding originated in a dance culture that translated poetic images of feet and footwear into visual feasts and sensory experiences accessible to all.

When Tang poets waxed lyrical about silk slippers and maidens treading on water or lotus blossoms, chances are they were referring to a dance performance they had watched at official banquets, in private homes, or on the

FIGURE 16

Ensemble of Daoist goddesses crossing a bridge that spans a lotus pond. This segment depicts some of the musical instruments popular in Tang court and society. *Procession of Immortals Paying Homage to the Primordial* (Chaoyuan xianzhang tu). Wu Zongyuan, fl. early 11th century, long scroll, ink on silk. From *Chinese Costumes*, p. 219, pl. 175.

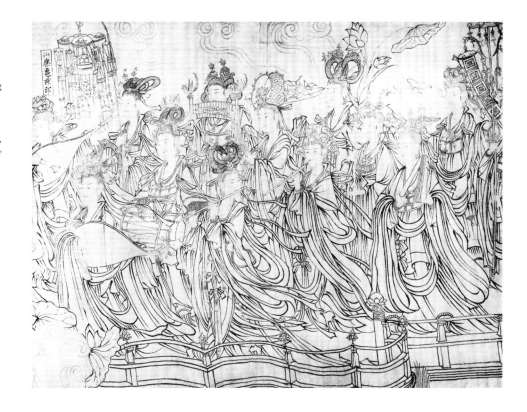

streets. The Tang was the golden age of both poetry and dance in Chinese history. Traditional dances, developed as part of Confucian court ceremonies, featured formulaic steps set to slow and monotonous drum beats and bell chimes. The sober tone of the performance reflects the high regard Confucius had for the didactic value of dance: the movement of the dancer's body harmonizes forces in heaven and earth; the solemnity is said to have the power to inspire the audience to mend their ways and become better sons and ministers. Although spellbinding, this kind of dance was performed only at the most formal state functions before small audiences. Tang courtiers and com-moners alike were mesmerized by a different kind of dance culture that came from India and Persia via the Silk Road. Dance was just one of the many exotic tastes in visual culture and cuisine that merchants and entertainers from Central Asia, India, and Southeast Asia introduced to Tang China when they settled in the capital and trading depots in the provinces.

A genre of military dance that involved up to one hundred twenty men dressed in armor and wielding sabers became popular. The early Tang emperors, celebrating the quelling of the land, had high officials compose the lyrics and stage these so-called Broken Battle Formations dance ensembles during festivals to rouse the troops and the people. These performances, a medieval equivalent of the modern military parade, transformed dance from a courtly affair into a public gala. The Broken Battle Formations dances were so popular that they became known in India and were staged in Japan, which adopted many elements of Tang culture for its own use. Military dances of all sorts, from calisthenic ensembles to solitary swordswomen performing on street corners, captivated Chinese audiences. Coincidentally, the lion dance, the climax of Chinese new year celebrations worldwide today, became popu-lar as a temple routine during the Tang. Outfitted in colorful pants and rid-ing boots, performers of these dances could not have had bound feet.

In addition to the virile battle formations, entertainers from Central Asia injected a heavy dose of sensuality into Chinese dance. Some of the foreign dances were deemed too risqué for Chinese tastes—such as those featuring dancers with naked torsos and limbs—and soon fell into disfavor. But other elements, especially tunes with fast lilting rhythms played on string and woodwind instruments, caught on. The aesthetics of some of the foreign female dancers, with an elongated silhouette of slender waist and tight long sleeves that hugged the arms and trailed long trains, introduced a sensuous and feminine sensibility to Chinese dance. When an ensemble of female

dancers swirled their arms, their fluttering sleeves must have reminded viewers of the ribbons that announced the approach of the Goddess of the River
Luo. A poetic image had come alive.

Exotic militancy and sensuality were combined in a female dance known
by the foreign name "Tazhi," the Tang term for present-day Tadzhikistan, situated north of Afghanistan. Rapid drum beats would announce the solo or
duet dancers. Sometimes the pair of young girls performing the duet would
enter the stage hidden in a huge lotus; as the petals opened the dancers would
begin a slow segment that showcased their willowy waists. The pace would
pick up as the dancers launched into acrobatic steps not found in Chinese
dances—thrusting arms, swirling body, leaping, or stomping feet in pace with
the quickening music. They would be dressed in Central Asian costume—
pillbox hat festooned with tiny bells, colorful dress with waist girdled in, and
brocade riding boots. Following Persian fashion, their eyebrows would be
thickly painted, and a henna ornament adorned their foreheads. The Tazhi
became the single most popular foreign dance in Tang China; Chinese dancers
called Tazhi girls soon learned the art and performed in military camps, official family receptions, and licensed entertainment quarters throughout the
empire. Viewers were enchanted by the chiming bells, the combination of willowy flexibility with gymnastic prowess, and the come-hither eyes of the
dancers.[7]

Partly in reaction to the virile style of military dances, Chinese artists
developed a new repertoire in which the dancers wore dancing slippers
rather than boots, which originated from the horse riders in the steppes. One
example is the Dragon Pond, an early eighth-century court dance named
after a pond in the reigning emperor's former residence. The twelve dancers,
dressed in five-colored gauze robes and Chinese dancing slippers (styled
"carefree"), appeared slowly with headdresses shaped like lotus blossoms.
Both the footwear and the music, a variation of proper court music, marked a

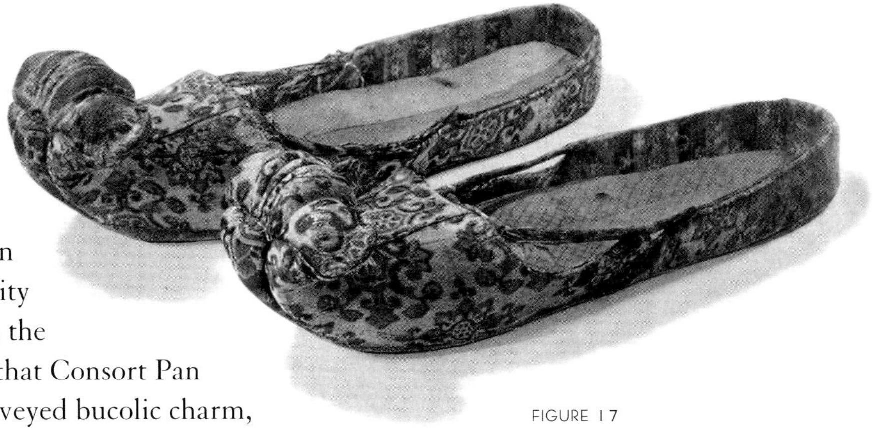

deliberate attempt to depart from the pervasive Central Asian influence at the time. The dress simulated the glistening water of a lotus pond, whereas the headdress appeared to the dazzled viewer to be lotus blossoms floating on water.[8] This was yet another example of the Chinese spin on the Indian lotus symbol, evoking the tranquility of the ubiquitous lotus pond found in gardens in the warm temperate south. Unlike the golden lotus that Consort Pan trod on, the lotus in the Dragon Pond dance conveyed bucolic charm, not wanton lust.

FIGURE 17
Cloud-tip male shoes from a Tang-dynasty tomb in Astana, outside the city of Turfan. White silk upper with blue and brown floral medallion motifs. Both the upper and lining were made of *jin*-brocade woven in the traditional technique of warp-faced patterning. Length: 29.7 cm (11¼ in.), Tang dynasty (618–907). From *Chinese Costumes*, p. 251, pl. 205.

The most popular dance that signaled the "Chinese turn" is the Rainbow Skirt and Feathered Cape, believed to be composed by the Tang emperor Xuanzong (r. 712–56) for his favorite consort, Yang Guifei (700–55). Known as Jade Ring Yang, she was China's Helen of Troy. Her famously voluptuous body set a new standard of beauty for women throughout the empire. The emperor was so enamoured of her that he became lax in his duties. When a general rebelled, the emperor fled the capital with his consort. At the shabby depot of Mawei his guards mutinied, demanding Guifei's head. The heart-broken emperor put his lover to death and eventually was restored to the throne. Although the empire was to survive another century and a half, the rebellion tipped the balance between royal and regional forces; historians concur that it signaled the beginning of the end. Consort Yang lived on as the most famous femme fatale in Chinese drama, poetry, and novels.

The Rainbow Skirt and Feathered Cape also became legendary. Set to Chinese strings and woodwind music with a humming chorus, this slow courtly dance was performed solo or in groups. The considerable body of the lead dancer was further weighed down by an oversized chignon and headdress, a cape evoking feathered clouds, and "cloud-tip" slippers with a dramatic cloudlike upturned toe. The gentle swirling of the dancer's sleeves and skirt along with fluttering ornaments on the headdress mesmerized romantic rulers and poets. The appeal of the dance lay not in athletic skills but in an ephemeral grace paced by delicate footwork.

A popular song of the time, preserved by sheer accident in the Dunhuang caves in the northwestern desert, described Consort Yang's countenance from her head down. After lingering on her hair, eyebrows, eyes, lips, breast, dress, and fragrance, the song focuses on her feet, clad in footwear even more dramatic than the cloud-tip slipper: "[The dancer] soars on clogs with stilts ["teeth"]; lazily she scuffs her step; haltingly she shuffles her two feet."[9] The picture of the dancer languishing in dainty steps, although just as attractive, presents a bodily image that is the opposite of the agile athleticism of the Tazhi girls. During the Tang, the two styles coexisted, but eventually the style embodied by Consort Yang won out.

So influential were the aesthetics of the consort's Rainbow Skirt dance that oversized chignons, cloudlike capes, shawl-like ribbons draped on forearms,

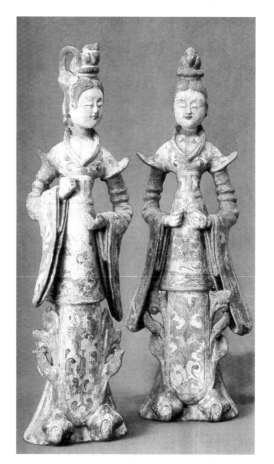

FIGURE 18
Painted clay figurines. Both stylish ladies have high chignons, layered garments with low-cut collars, and prominent cloud-tip shoes. Tang dynasty (618–907). From *Chinese Costumes*, p. 212, pl. 171.

and hefty body types became the norm of Tang fashion in the second half of the eighth century. So, too, were hesitant small footsteps hidden under long draping skirts. In this way, the fated consort prefigured the bodily aesthetics of footbinding. As legend would have it, Yang left behind a brocade sock in Mawei, the place of her death. An old granny chanced upon it by the roadside and proceeded to charge passers-by for a peep.[10] Although the lost sock recalls the Chinese Cinderella story and suggests to some later readers that the consort's feet must have been tiny, the truth is that Consort Yang could not have had bound feet. But as the Rainbow Skirt and Feathered Cape dance remained popular for two centuries after her death, dainty and slow footsteps gradually became the only way for a woman to conduct herself.

After the Fall, the Music Continued

Two types of bodily culture were thus in vogue during the Tang. On the one hand, the popularity of the Tazhi and other military dances that required dancers to wear riding boots created an atmosphere antithetical to footbinding. On the other hand, the Rainbow Skirt dance presented a more courtly and Chinese cultural alternative. After the Tang empire collapsed and the Chinese rejected Central Asian elements in their national culture, narrow feet and dainty steps became de rigueur as riding boots and stomping feet suddenly looked ridiculously barbaric.

Although the robust militant style went out of fashion, the sensuality embodied by Central Asian dancers remained salient in Chinese culture and literature. After the Tang capital in the north was overrun by foreign soldiers, court musicians, poets, and dancers were dispersed throughout the empire. Many regrouped in the banquet halls and pleasure quarters that sprang up in the southern cities during the early years of the Northern Song dynasty (960–1127), founded by a Chinese general who quelled the foreign soldiers and steered the country into a renaissance of Han Chinese culture. It was most likely in those pleasure houses that literati from all over the empire en route to the civil service exam came face to face with beguiling entertainers scuffing in silk slippers. Some returned home with one or several of these girls, installing them as household entertainers or concubines. Although there is no proof for this, I found myself picturing the legal wife watching the singing and dancing in her reception room. Enraged (or enchanted, who knows?), she retreated to the boudoir and rummaged her storage chest for remnants of brocade to make new shoes and strips of gauze to swaddle her toes.

Perhaps the most popular and convincing origin myth is that of Yaoniang, a dancer in the court of Li Yü (937–78, r. 961–74), the Last Sovereign of the Southern Tang kingdom, one of the regional regimes vying for the throne after the collapse of the Tang empire. Our full version of her story comes from a fourteenth-century book: "Yaoniang is a slender beauty who excelled in dancing. The Last Sovereign had a golden lotus built. The six-foot tall lotus was festooned with precious stones and fine ribbons on the inside, creating a magnificent blossom of variegated colors. He then had Yaoniang swaddle her feet with gauze cloth so that they were slender and small, curving upward in the shape of the new moon. Clad only in socks she danced in the clouds, swirling as if she were soaring into the sky.... Many sought to imitate her, admiring as they did the slender arch."[11] The prop of a human-size lotus reminds us of the Tazhi girls, whereas the swirling and soaring recalls the Chinese lotus dances. Most striking, however, is the upwardly curved crescent shape of Yaoniang's feet, which we have already found on the upper-class ladies from the thirteenth-century tombs.

The story of Yaoniang was the first origin myth that mentioned specifically the use of gauze binders and the crescent-shaped feet. Also significant is the seemingly minor detail of her dancing "clad only in socks," presumably over the binders—Consort Yang's top-heavy cloud-tip slipper was shed, giving way to a footwear and motion similar to modern ballet. Yaoniang may

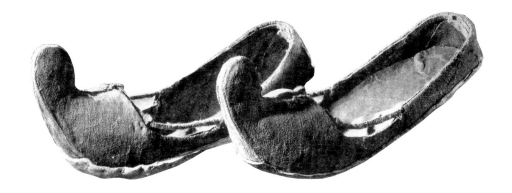

FIGURE 19
Evolution of footwear.

From top:
These Tang-dynasty male shoes
are made of hemp with a leather-
reinforced sole. Excavated from
Astana, Turfan area. Length: 25 cm
(9⅞ in.), Tang dynasty (618–907).
From *Chinese Costumes*, p. 253,
pl. 207.

The crescent shape of cloud-tip shoes
might have inspired the shoes for
bound feet found in Song-dynasty
tombs, such as Lady Huang Sheng's
(see fig. 10, p. 21).

not have been a historical figure—
there is no mention of her in the
masterful song-lyrics that the Last
Sovereign left behind—but there surely were
plenty of dancers in the Southern Tang kingdom. Situated in the wealthy heartland of
South China, it was the mecca of music and
dance culture in the tenth century. The Last Sovereign's senior queen Zhou, a
historical figure, was an expert of the Rainbow Skirt and Feathered Cape
dance who was credited with artistic innovations. Authentic or not, Yaoniang
fits so well into what we know of footbinding that she might as well have
been invented. Indeed, we would not be far off if we think of her as a stand-
in for thousands of dancing girls whose sensuality every patriarch of the
house secretly longed for but only dukes and kings in Southland could afford.

The birth of footbinding is a centuries-long process. A lyrical ideal centering on the tread of nymphs and maidens was born as early as the third century and became popular in the fifth and sixth centuries; by the ninth century a Cinderella complex was evident in the storytelling tradition. Around the same time, Central Asian dancers brought new aesthetic tastes to the cosmopolitan Tang people, transforming the Chinese body culture in favor of female sensuality. The literary ideal became an actual bodily practice only after the Tang empire collapsed, when crescent-shaped feet and dainty steps acquired new cachet as symbols of a Chinese cultural renaissance.

The many paradoxes involved in this story point to the inherently contradictory nature of footbinding. Nurtured by a hybrid cosmopolitan Tang culture, footbinding later became quintessentially Chinese. Also ironic is the fact that in the beginning the practice was meant not to cripple but to enhance the grace of the dancer. After its birth, its meaning shifted dramatically, even though the original hint of sensuality did not entirely disappear and remained on the margins of respectable discourse—in ribald folk songs and the ars erotica, for example. Hence the contradictory image of footbinding in history as at once degenerate and virtuous, grotesque and refined. This contradiction is embodied in the key symbol for footbinding—the lotus blossom, being both a Buddhist sign of piety and a poetic allusion to sensory pleasures ranging from erotic to bucolic.

It is undeniable that footbinding was born of a male fantasy that turned women into objects of their amorous desires. As natural as these desires may be, if left unchecked they threaten to destroy the harmony in family and society. This is why from the start there is an unseemly undercurrent to footbinding: moralists for whom sex was only good for procreation repeatedly chastised Han Wo and many poets of *Among the Flowers*. In the late eleventh century, in one of the earliest references to footbinding as a practice, scholar Xu Zhi (1028–1103) praised a widow who "cannot spare a moment to bind her two feet, / her only concern is putting the four limbs to good use."[12] For as long as it lasted, footbinding was condemned as a frivolous pursuit that distracted the family son and daughter from productive uses of their bodies. Such is the Janus-faced nature of footbinding that the impulse that brought it into being cannot account for its spread and long history, which is essentially a history of domestication. As it migrated from the palace to respectable households, the blatant sensuality had to be draped in the mantle of domestic values.

During this evolution housewives and mothers gave footbinding an entirely new set of meanings, as a celebration of women's work and mother-hood. In this book we do not have the space to trace the history of the prac-tice in the ars erotica. But in the chapters that follow we will examine how the meaning of footbinding underwent a sea change when it was incorpo-rated into the Confucian cult of domesticity, thereby changing the lives not only of a few dancers but also of millions of women.

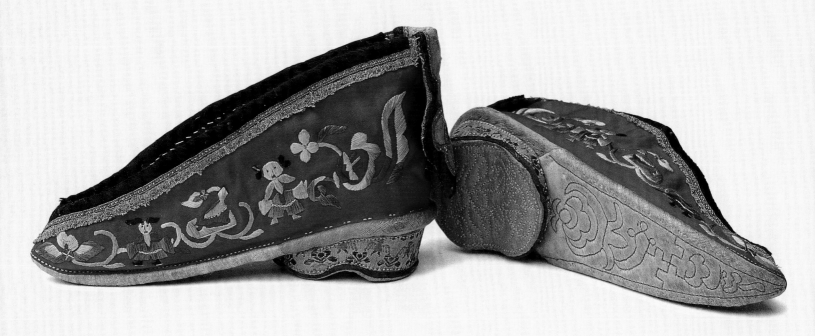

FIGURE 20
Southern-style shoes in red silk. On the side of the upper the wish for many children is expressed by a visual pun: lotus (*lian*, also "continuous"); mouth organ (*sheng*, also "give birth to"); children. Length: 16 cm (6¼ in.), 20th century. BSM S01.5.AB.

FIGURE 21, OPPOSITE
Children's tiger shoes, all handmade by women in the twentieth century.

Left to right:
Beige and black silk tiger shoe. Length: 14.4 cm (5⅝ in.). BSM S83.88.A.

Royal blue tiger shoe with green eyes. Length: 15.5 cm (6⅛ in.). BSM P92.139.A.

Maroon velvet tiger shoe with rabbit fur ruff. Length: 15 cm (5⅞ in.). BSM S93.14.A.

Red satin tiger shoe with two turquoise pompoms. Length: 13.4 cm (5¼ in.). BSM S87.3.A.

Greyish blue tiger shoe with small black ruffle. Length: 15 cm (5⅞ in.). BSM S80.1073.A.

CHAPTER 2

THE TIES THAT BIND

*There are three offenses to filial piety,
and the most serious is depriving your family of posterity.*
— MENCIUS

Rarely does one pass by a Chinese house, garden, or restaurant without hearing the sound of children. The Chinese love of children is legendary, and colorful folkways have sprung up to ensure their safe passage to adulthood. One scheme allots an individual one of the twelve so-called zodiac animals according to the year of birth, and the newborn is draped in hats, capes, or shoes with the emblem—a tiger, a dragon, or a ram (see "Ancient Zodiac Animals"). Avoid harm by knowing your place in the complex constellation of cosmological forces; the message is loud and clear. And those who live to a ripe old age deserve privileges because they must have done something right.

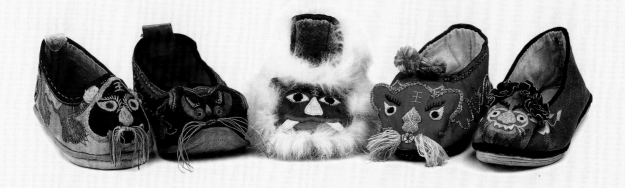

ANCIENT ZODIAC ANIMALS

The zodiac animals are products of the sophisticated knowledge of the stars that the ancient Chinese possessed. They appeared in almanacs as early as the third century BCE, two hundred years after Confucius. The twelve animals corresponded to the day of a person's birth—not the year (there were thirty days in a month, a quarter of a twelve-by-ten-day cycle.) Parents were advised to name the child after the animal—Dragon Gongsun—or after attributes of the animal—Victorious Gongsun. The underlying belief is not a fatalistic attitude that one's future is predetermined by fate. To the contrary, the zodiac animals promote a proactive attitude in life: know yourself and the forces that shape you, and you can then make wise decisions for yourself and your family. The practice of identifying one's year of birth with a calendrical animal became popular in the sixth century and is still customary today.

TWELVE-YEAR CYCLES OF ZODIAC ANIMALS

Rat	1900	1912	1924	1936	1948	1960	1972	1984	1996	2008
Ox	1901	1913	1925	1937	1949	1961	1973	1985	1997	2009
Tiger	1902	1914	1926	1938	1950	1962	1974	1986	1998	2010
Rabbit	1903	1915	1927	1939	1951	1963	1975	1987	1999	2011
Dragon	1904	1916	1928	1940	1952	1964	1976	1988	2000	2012
Snake	1905	1917	1929	1941	1953	1965	1977	1989	2001	2013
Horse	1906	1918	1930	1942	1954	1966	1978	1990	2002	2014
Ram	1907	1919	1931	1943	1955	1967	1979	1991	2003	2015
Monkey	1908	1920	1932	1944	1956	1968	1980	1992	2004	2016
Rooster	1909	1921	1933	1945	1957	1969	1981	1993	2005	2017
Dog	1910	1922	1934	1946	1958	1970	1982	1994	2006	2018
Pig	1911	1923	1935	1947	1959	1971	1983	1995	2007	2019

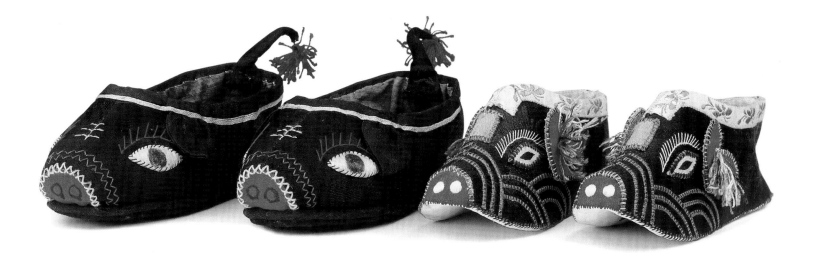

Respect for elders and love for children constituted the foundation of Chinese ethics, and this emphasis on continuity has clearly worked: the Chinese family as we know it first took shape during the Han dynasty, two millennia ago, and its basic structure and values are to a large extent still thriving today (see "Confucian Family Values"). The strength of the family creates special opportunities and constraints for men and women alike, and to understand why footbinding became an attractive option for women—leading to its spread from door to door from the twelfth century on—we have to begin by examining the place of daughters in the family.

FIGURE 22
Children's pig shoes, both pairs handmade by women in the twentieth century.

Left to right:
Length: 12.5 cm (4 ⅞ in.),
BSM P00.118.AB.

Length: 12 cm (4 ¾ in.),
BSM S97.153.AB.

Being a Girl in a Male World

It is often said that girls were second-class citizens in the traditional Chinese family, which is a classic case of a "patriarchy"—where power and responsibilities were handed down from father to son. This picture is not wrong but misleading. Boys and girls were often equally loved, but forces larger than human emotions dictated that boys were *valued* more. To ensure peace and harmony, the Chinese family established clear rules for passing on property, ritual responsibilities, and authority along the male line—from grandfather to father to son. Scholars have called this type of family "*patri*-lineal" and "*patri*-archal"; the root "patri" in both words signals a focus on males. The intent was not so much to discriminate against women, as is often taken to be, but to prevent family assets from falling into the hands of the families of the sons' wives. Unlike our society in which individuals own their houses and cars, in traditional China, strictly speaking, it was the family as a whole—not the sons—that owned houses and land, if any. The wealthiest families thus functioned more as a corporation jealously guarding its assets from hostile takeovers by its marital relatives.

The popular image that parents slighted their own daughters as outsiders is valid in theory. Given the patrilineal nature of the family, a woman did not have a permanent place in society until she married and had her name entered on the genealogy of her husband's family. But this image of the daughter as a devalued outsider in her parents' house is a far cry from the experience of most daughters. The historical record is full of diaries of fathers who doted on their girls by teaching them how to read. Human feelings aside, parents had real incentives to raise a healthy and good daughter who would fetch a high bride price. Although daughters were not supposed to inherit family property, they often received jewelry as dowry, which made brides, ironically, the only party in a family who had private holdings. If the family was wealthy, this kind of informal inheritance could be substantial.

CONFUCIAN FAMILY VALUES

The Chinese family is a living tree. If the climate and soil conditions are right, young branches thrive and buds blossom. Having seen to the healthy growth of the tender shoots by sheltering them from the sun and rain, the old branches would eventually die off. Softly they fall onto the earth—"a fallen leaf returns to the roots," as a proverb says—initiating another cycle of birth and rebirth. Gone but not forgotten, the fallen leaves and stems supply nutrients for the living, just as the memories of grandpa and grandma sustain the young. If old and new, stem and branch, pull together and each does its part, the family tree will prosper, casting a soothing shade on the entire neighborhood for generations to come.

The biggest difference between the normative traditional Chinese family and that in the modern West is that Chinese boys and girls learned from a tender age that the health of the living tree took precedence over individual happiness. It is not that the Chinese did not believe in "individualism"; there was plenty of room for personal growth and private pleasures. But the Chinese sages thought that a broken branch or leaf is weak and less likely to fulfill its full potential. To be part of a whole, that is the condition of being human.

Through the centuries, the trunk of the tree gains another ring, and its tip reaches for the sky as its roots sink deeper and deeper into the soil. Similarly, a family prospers only if it remains rooted in the land. For its members every journey from home is an exile; every day spent on the road is a distraction from life's biggest joy. Today, we who celebrate mobility and speed may find this preference for rootedness limiting and old-fashioned. We should not overlook, however, that the Chinese devotion to a stable and sedentary life offers every family member a deep sense of security. Not only does one always know where one belongs; there is also the assurance of a safety net in case of personal failings.

According to Confucian thinking, a healthy and upright family is the foundation of a civilized country. A filial son will grow to be a good citizen, and a loyal wife sets an example for the public official, who is thought of as the helpmate of kings. This is another difference between the ideal traditional Chinese family and the modern one—the former is not a private haven separate from the state; it is in fact a microcosm of the state and the center of the public sphere. A mother who teaches her children well is the linchpin of a moral society and a peaceful country.

There are many stories that tell of a wife pawning her jewelry to bail out a husband in dire straits.

Marriage is of paramount importance for the families and individuals concerned. The groom's family gained a productive member and a potential mother; the daughter gained a home and a socially respectable identity—wife. She and her parents would want to make her as attractive as possible in order to marry well, into an economically secure family with kind in-laws. The standards for a good bride varied over time and by geographical location, and elite families often held to different standards from those of the socially deprived. Generally speaking, in the early years of the Tang when aristocratic families held sway in politics, marriage was a form of political alliance and pedigree was key. When politics became more democratic and officials were chosen on the basis of merit during the Song dynasty, personal attributes became more common in the selection of brides. Moral repute—signified by a pair of bound feet—later became a common requirement. By the sixteenth century, a sophisticated education was added on top of morality, and an ideal bride had to be both talented in literature and virtuous. In the nineteenth century, ironically on the eve of the practice's decline, a pair of bound feet became an overriding factor among bride seekers in lower-class families.

Footbinding spread from the thirteenth to fifteenth century because it enhanced a daughter's marriage prospects, as is often said. But the reason for the desirability of brides with bound feet is not, as is sometimes assumed, that parents gave in to their son's wishes for a sexually attractive wife. An openly seductive bride threatened family harmony, and in any case sons did not have any say over the choice of a spouse. Marriage was a family-to-family affair, to be decided by parents who knew better. In fact, future in-laws desired brides with bound feet because it signaled not sexuality but modesty and morality. More than marriage prospects, the biggest reason for the domestication of footbinding was its association with women's textile work, which enjoyed

FIGURE 23
A group of wedding shoes.

Clockwise from top:
Taiwan-style wedding shoes in plain red satin. Length: 10 cm (4 in.), 20th century. Collection of Dr. Chi-sheng Ko.

Taiwan-style wedding shoes in embroidered red satin. Length: 9.3 cm (3⅝ in.), 20th century. Collection of Dr. Chi-sheng Ko.

Southern-style wedding shoes in red silk and decorated with golden and silver couching. Length: 15.4 cm (6⅛ in.), 20th century. BSM P01.3.

Northern-style wedding shoes in red silk. Paper-cut gold leaf decoration affixed to sole. Length: 15.8 cm (6¼ in.), 20th century. Collection of Dr. Chi-sheng Ko.

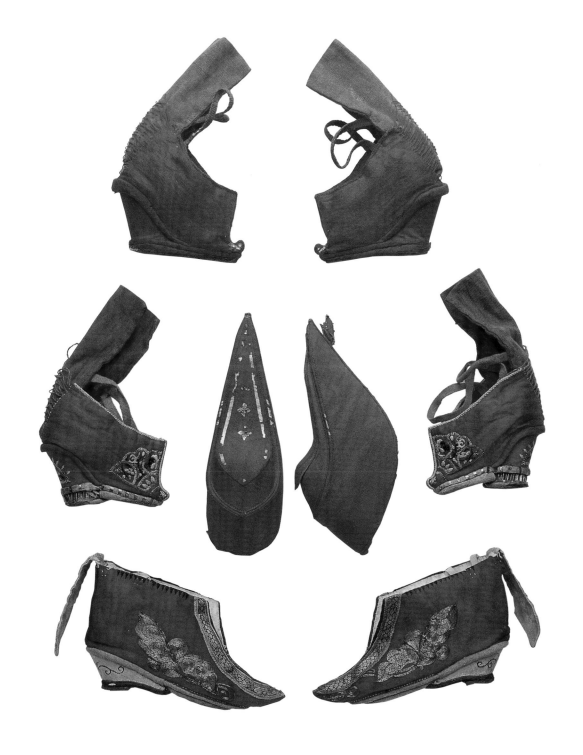

high cultural and economic value in a Confucian society. We will examine this more closely in the next chapter when we visit the women's workroom and learn how they spun, wove, and made shoes. Here we would leave aside abstract analysis about the family and head to the inner chambers of the Chinese house (see "The Chinese House, Where Women Ruled the Roost"). To teach her girl how to be a woman in a man's world, a mother is about to bind her daughter's feet.

Becoming a Woman

The daughter's first binding took place in the depths of the women's quarters under the direction of her mother, sometimes assisted by grandmothers and aunts; no men were privy to the ceremonial process. It was a solemn occasion marking the girl's coming of age, the first step of her decade-long grooming to become a bride—a prelude to a sweet-sixteen party. A sense of anticipation stirred the women's hearts, tinted with a bittersweet awareness that as women, they could gain power only by way of their bodies. Their physical and bodily labor—in the silkworm hut as in the childbirth chamber—was what made them valuable to the family. This message would soon be inscribed on the daughter's very body. The pain of footbinding anticipated the pain of childbirth, the blessing and curse for a Chinese woman.

As if to underscore the message that binding—like labor—is a fact of a woman's life, the materials and tools needed were not specialized gadgets but everyday items already in use in the women's rooms. These include such sewing implements as scissors, needles, and thread—the former for trimming the toenails and the latter for sealing the binders tight. The binding cloth would have been woven afresh. For adult women the average size of the cloth is about 10 cm wide by 4 meters long (4 inches by 13 feet), but the length varies. Women wove the cloth and stored it in a roll, like fresh bandages, ready to be torn off at the desired length. Alum powder, an astringent,

FIGURE 24
Tools for binding feet.

Clockwise from left:
Rolls of binding cloth, in white and dyed colors. 20th century. BSM P01.5.

Jar of medicinal foot powder, assembled in contemporary Taiwan using an ancient recipe. Collection of Dr. Chi-sheng Ko.

Bamboo cage for fuming binding cloth. 19th century. Collection of Dr. Chi-sheng Ko.

Sewing scissors. 19th century. BSM P01.22.

Box of fragrant foot powder sold in emporiums. Early 20th century. Collection of Dr. Chi-sheng Ko.

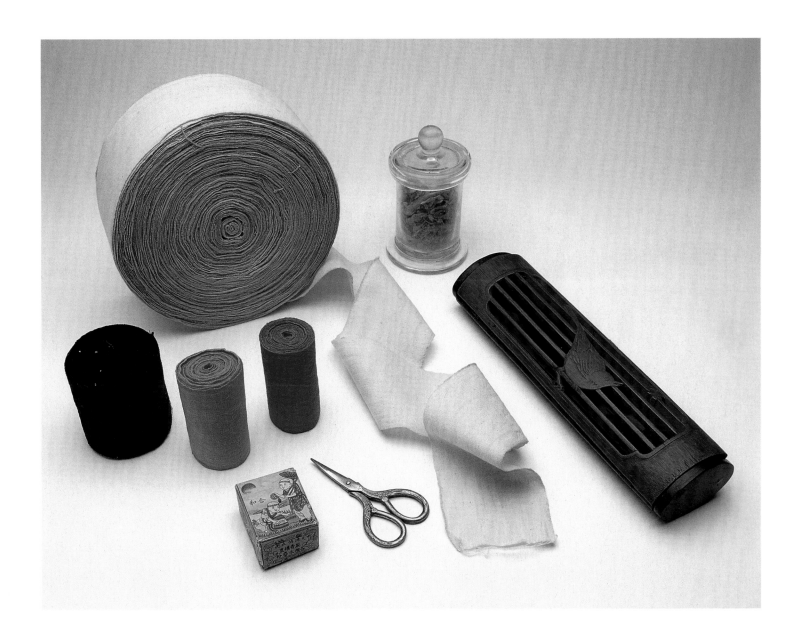

THE CHINESE HOUSE, WHERE WOMEN RULED THE ROOST

The Chinese house is more than a place to live. It is alive, a space animated with the spirits of ancestors and cosmic energies. It is also a school, teaching a boy or girl by nonverbal means how to behave according to Confucian norms.

The house is wrought of two types of architecture—a material one and an imaginary one superimposed on the wood-and-earth structure. There are three imaginary architectures: the space of decorum, an embodiment of Confucian values; the space of cosmic energy, captured in the art of *fengshui* (geomancy or siting; literally, "wind and water"); and the space of culture, representing Chinese views of home and shelter. Being human is to live and work in a house, not on the road or in the wilderness.*

The house is a microcosm of the human world and the universe. The basic format of a Han Chinese house—a courtyard lined with living quarters enclosed in high walls—is duplicated in every region and used for palaces, schools, temples, and offices alike. This remarkable uniformity reflects a fundamental Chinese worldview that a family in the house is the moral building block of the empire, part of the natural order of the universe. The imperial palace is but a fancy house built on the identical principles as a peasant house. Indeed, the emperor is the father of the people and the "son of heaven."

The house is the women's domain. Marginal to the formal family structure, women are masters of the house. A second-century Confucian classic, the *Book of Rites*, prescribed an ideal division of labor for society:

"Men manage the outer, women manage the inner." Specifically, the latter includes being in charge of the food and wine, which means not only the daily meals but also the ritually proper supplication in ceremonies honoring the ancestors and the gods. In the house women were not only custodians of domestic morality—industry and frugality—they were also household managers in the practical sense. Among the most visible powers wielded by women is the "power of the key" to the domestic bursar. After years of tutelage the bride would eventually inherit the key from her ailing mother-in-law. In theory, the male head of household controls the family resources, but in practice his wife keeps the account books and makes decisions about the household budget.

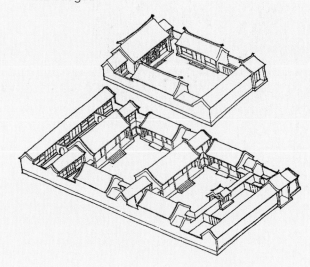

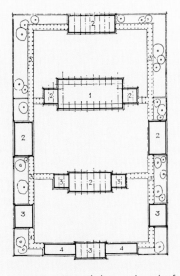

In the modern West, where domesticity is often likened to a prison and women have fought long and hard for equal opportunities in the workplace, it is tempting to regard the Chinese housewife, no matter how well provided for, as a cloistered creature deprived of life choices. Yet this is not the way Chinese women viewed themselves before the nineteenth century. In the Confucian world, the family—and by extension the domestic life—enjoyed much higher prestige and importance than in our society. Without having to set foot out of her door, a housewife and mother could work hard to make the world a better place. And there is no better place to start than her daughter's feet.

---

* The concept of "imaginary architecture" is Klaas Ruitenbeek's. See his *Carpentry and Building in Late Imperial China* (Leiden: E.J. Brill, 1993), p. 62. Francesca Bray has expounded on the three spaces of decorum, cosmic energy, and culture in *Technology and Gender: Fabrics of Power in Late Imperial China* (Berkeley: University of California Press, 1997). For the elaborate scheme of symbols for happiness embedded in the house, see Ronald G. Knapp, *China's Living Houses: Folk Beliefs, Symbols, and Household Ornamentation* (Honolulu: University of Hawaii Press, 1999).

1 Great Vermilion Bird Road
2 Imperial city
3 Palace city
4 West market
5 East market
6 Daming gong
7 West imperial park
8 Pond

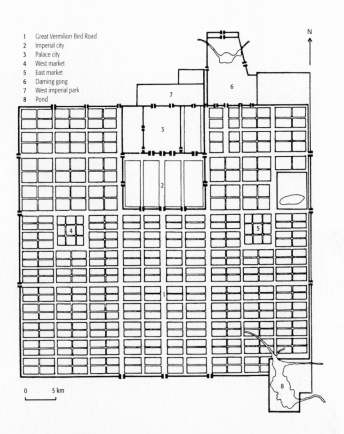

Hierarchical space, showing similar principle of spatial organization from courtyard house to imperial city planning (left to right). From Lothar Ledderose, *Ten Thousand Things*, pp. 113, 116, 136.

would be sprinkled in between the toes. Fragrant powder from the toiletry chest dusted the cloth and the lining of the shoe. Ancient herbal formulas for medicinal powder or tonic, made specially to soften the bones or to speed up the healing, were passed on from family to family. Dating as early as the Song dynasty, these formulas remained popular until modern times, attesting to the meticulous care that women from well-off families received.

Although many of the implements needed for the first binding were readily available, new shoes would have to be made specially for the daughter. Months before the auspicious day the mother and elder women in the house began to prepare an array of tiny shoes for the girl, for daytime training and for bed. In Taiwan, where only settler families from southern Fujian (Min-nan in Chinese) bound their daughters' feet, mothers followed Fujian custom in making a series of training shoes with a rather odd appearance. Sometimes called "toad shoes" because of their shape, they became progressively smaller in size and higher in the heel. The wooden heels were left uncovered because these shoes were worn strictly behind closed doors, for the purpose of teaching the newly bound girl how to shift weight and walk with a shuffling gait. In other regions, mothers would simply make several pairs of regular shoes progressively smaller in size.

A typical age for binding to start was five to six years old. As infants, boys and girls mingled freely in the house; children were considered gender-neutral in many ways. Boys and girls led more segregated lives as they came of age, which according to Chinese thinking was the time when they became capable of understanding sexual matters. For families who could afford the loss of potential labor force, the boy would be sent to school and the girl would have her feet bound. Ritual convention dictated that a boy came of age when he turned eight by Chinese count and a girl, seven. This is because *The Yellow Emperor's Classic of Internal Medicine*, a classic medical treatise, suggested that boys developed in cycles of eight years, whereas girls' cycles

STEPS IN BINDING

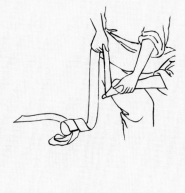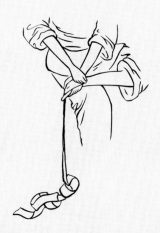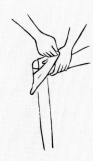

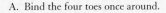

FIGURE 25
Adapted from Howard S. Levy,
Chinese Footbinding, pp. 24–25.

A. Bind the four toes once around.

B. Then pull the binding cloth toward the outside; turn it toward the sole, folding the four toes toward the underside of the arch.

C. From the inside of the foot, pull the binding toward the front point and turn it tightly around the big toe.

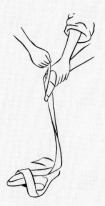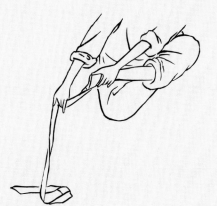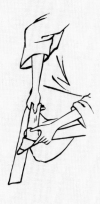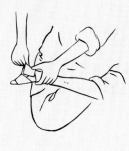

D. Wrap the heel from the outer side of the foot, and pull the binding cloth toward the front point. Wrap the front, except for the big toe.

E. Wrap over the instep, go around the ankle, and return to the instep.

F. Turn toward the heel and wrap the binding cloth from the inner side of the foot to the front point.

G. Wrap from the inner side and over the instep to the outer side. Wrap around the heel and pull the binding cloth back toward the instep.

FIGURE 26
Adapted from Ko, Chi-sheng, *Shengui hongyan lei*, p. 28.

Footbinding had three physical effects on the foot:

1. Shortening the length of the foot

2. Reshaping the sole of the foot, producing an arched bulge on the instep and a deep crevice on the underside of the arch

3. Reducing the width of the sole

The reshaping of the foot was achieved by the bending and stretching of the ligaments and tendons of the foot, shifting the placement of the bones as a result. Footbinding did not break the bones of the foot.

In specific terms, the arched bulge on the instep was made by bending the metatarsal bones downward and stretching the ligaments joining the metatarsals to the cuneiform and cuboid bones. These bones atrophied after prolonged binding. The deep crevice on the underside of the arch was made by pushing the calcaneus (heel bone) inward. As a result, the heel of the foot stood almost parallel with the fibula, the long outer bone of the lower leg, and at a right angle to the floor.

The body weight was born by three parts: the heel, where the achilles tendon joins the calcaneus; the tip of the first metatarsal; the third, fourth and fifth toes, which were folded under. A woman with bound feet walked with a shuffling gait. Her hip and thigh muscles, which propelled her motion, grew strong. Her lower leg between the knee and the ankle, however, atrophied from lack of use.

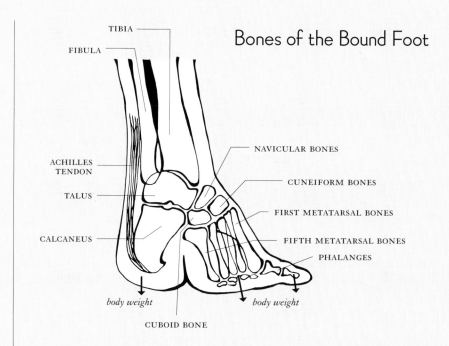

Bones of the Bound Foot

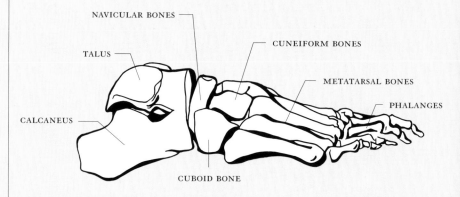

Bones of the Unbound Foot

measured seven years. Since the Chinese count age (*sui*) by taking the lunar year of one's birth as year one and adding a year at each lunar new year's day, a seven-*sui* girl would be around five or six years old by Western reckoning.[1]

Ritual formalities aside, the actual binding age tended to range from five to eight years old. For families that lived close to a hand-to-mouth existence, binding a daughter's feet was like setting aside a sum of its monthly income for the savings account—an investment in the future can only come at the expense of immediate sacrifice. Year after year peasant parents struggled to save up a little cushion so that they could afford to take their daughter out of the most strenuous forms of labor in the fields. This is why the lower one went down the social scale, the later the age for binding tended to become. For most poor daughters before the nineteenth century, however, the day never came. In a flash she grew old enough to marry and like her mother, she would marry a poor farmer.

A prepubescent girl might not have been fully aware that she was being prepared for sexual service to her future family, but she knew that footbinding was her initiation rite into the women's community, which consisted of her mother, maternal aunts, elder sisters, and cousins if they lived nearby. With her hair tied up in tufts and her feet bound, her attire signaled her new status as bride-in-waiting, almost a woman, even though her body had yet to change physically. The women's community is not so much secretive as invisible, hidden behind the formal structures of the male-centered family. If the father's power was all too apparent and the father-son tie was celebrated in concrete physical form—the ancestral shrine and the genealogy book, for example—women's power was informal and the mother-daughter tie was celebrated only in the women's hearts and minds.

In fact, instability and insecurity were the first facts of life that the mother had to teach the daughter. A woman's station in life was not fixed. Unlike her brothers, who were born into the same house they would eventually inherit

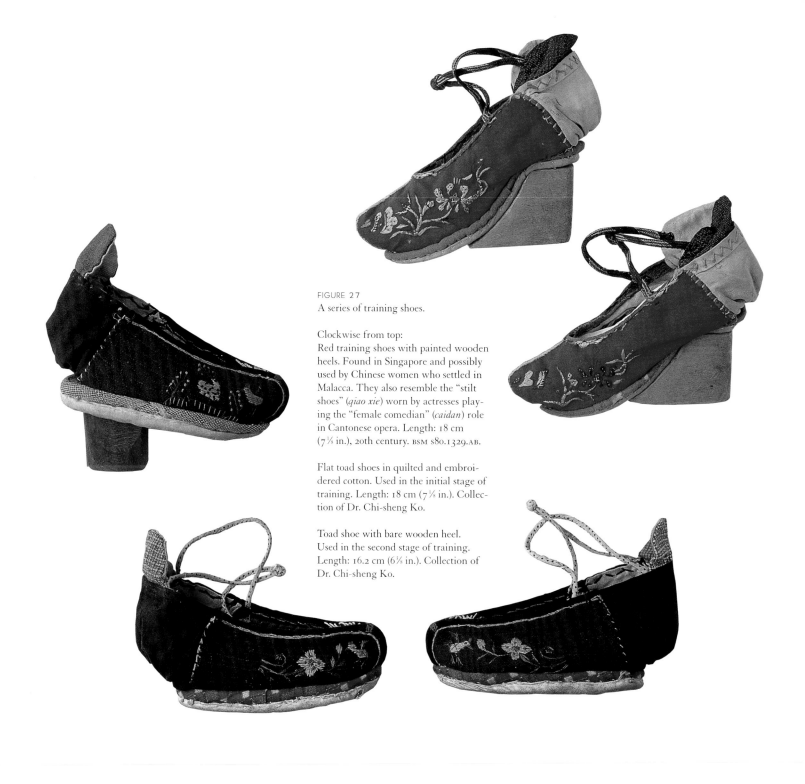

FIGURE 27

A series of training shoes.

Clockwise from top:
Red training shoes with painted wooden heels. Found in Singapore and possibly used by Chinese women who settled in Malacca. They also resemble the "stilt shoes" (*qiao xie*) worn by actresses playing the "female comedian" (*caidan*) role in Cantonese opera. Length: 18 cm (7⅛ in.), 20th century. BSM S80.1329.AB.

Flat toad shoes in quilted and embroidered cotton. Used in the initial stage of training. Length: 18 cm (7⅛ in.). Collection of Dr. Chi-sheng Ko.

Toad shoe with bare wooden heel. Used in the second stage of training. Length: 16.2 cm (6⅜ in.). Collection of Dr. Chi-sheng Ko.

and often die in, a girl had to rise up to new challenges in every stage of her life. The most traumatic dislocations she suffered were on her wedding day, when she entered a stranger's family, which she had to make her own. As she learned the idiosyncrasies of her mother-in-law, the most important person to please, she became more settled and comfortable. Her position became secure with the birth of a son; as the mother of sons she would gain a permanent and visible place in the family. As the mother of daughters she could only hope for the best.

Sons did not have an easier life—they were under intense pressure to succeed and not to let the family down. Nor were they free to pursue their own interests at the expense of the family business. Yet at least men in Chinese society had a basic choice—to work with the body or the mind; to be a worker or a scholar. For a woman, the body was her only gateway to a better future. To do textile work and to give birth—to attain value and meaning for herself, she could not do without the body. As a mother readied the training shoes and cloth binders for her daughter, both fruits of female labor, these thoughts might have raced through her head. Our bodies and labor make us women, she might have said to her daughter, and our bodies and labor are the ties that bind us in a female kinship that no men can undo.

Praying to the Tiny-Footed Maiden

As a crucial rite of passage for the daughter and a central event for the women's community, the binding of feet was rich in spiritual and religious meanings. To begin with, the day to begin binding had to be selected with care. Almanacs specifying auspicious days for the first binding can be found as early as the sixteenth century. In practice, the day and rituals varied a great deal from region to region, but the women's desire for perfect feet and the great length to which they were willing to go to achieve them, was universal.

For pragmatic reasons, the ideal season for binding to start was autumn, when feet were no longer sweaty and the breeze cooled off some of the discomfort. In Suzhou, a southern city famous for its elegant, elongated shoes for bound feet, binding customarily started with fanfare on the twenty-fourth day of the Eighth Moon. In honor of the Stove (or Kitchen) God, on that day women of the house would cook sticky rice, add red beans, shape the mixture into balls, and make offerings on the stove. The Stove God, ironically always a male, belongs to the male pantheon of celestial bureaucrats and presides over the line of patriarchs in the household. The offering of rice balls was a common ritual throughout China, for red beans were believed to have the power to ward off diseases and evil spirits. But in fashionable Suzhou the women added another layer of meaning to the ritual by designating the day the birthday of their goddess, the Tiny-Footed Maiden. When they made offerings to the Stove God, they also whispered a prayer to their goddess, wishing that their bones would be as soft as the rice ball and their feet as pretty as the Maiden's. A folk song describes the occasion:

> Misty is the white dew and full is the panicle of rice,
> The new rice ball, every family has tasted.
> Pity is the girl, hair newly tied in tufts,
> Trying on her first arched shoes, unsullied by dust.[2]

"White dew" is one of the twenty-four solar terms on the Chinese calendar and signals the slight chill of autumn that can turn dew into frost.

If there were statues or paintings made to honor the Tiny-Footed Maiden, they did not survive; hence we do not know what she looks like. Unlike the god of the stove, who was a public deity sanctioned by imperial decrees, the women's goddess was private and hidden, although no less "real" to the women because of it. We may picture the Maiden as the embodiment

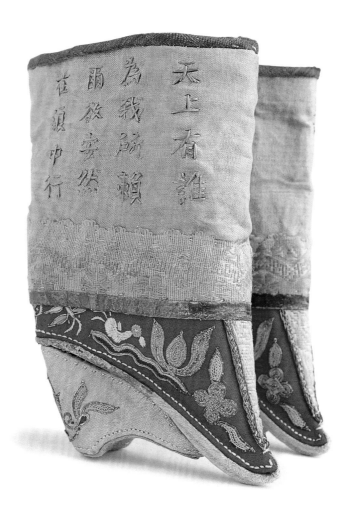

天上有誰
為我所賴
雨後安然
在浪中行

FIGURE 28
Shown actual size, tiny votive shoes
with embroidered prayer. The
prayer on the right shaft (shown)
reads: "Who on heaven, / Can I lean
on? / May you go in peace, / Across
the waves." On the left shaft: "May
god bless you, / 'Til we meet again, /
Meet again, / Meet again." Length:
5.7 cm (2¼ in.), late 19th century.
Collection of Vincent V. Comer.

of the collective aspirations of numerous mothers and daughters. Perhaps she even looked different to each of her devotees, as the projection of each girl's most cherished self.

More widespread than prayers to the Tiny-Footed Maiden were offerings made to the Bodhisattva Guanyin, the Buddhist goddess of mercy. In India, where Buddhism originated, the bodhisattva was depicted as a handsome man with a thin mustache. As he traveled to medieval China, he underwent a sex change and eventually appeared as a woman—often a mother figure—with boundless compassion. Her temples have dotted the Chinese landscape for centuries, even in the most remote corners. She promises immediate assistance to all who call upon her name or chant her prayers, regardless of sex, class, or creed. Although Guanyin has no lack of male followers, she is a special patron to countless mothers and daughters. One of her most important jobs is to grant children, and she remains as popular as ever today.[3]

In many regions of China, weeks before a girl was to start binding, her mother would make a pair of votive shoes and place them on the incense burner in the neighborhood Guanyin temple or on the altar of a makeshift shrine at home. Prayers were offered every day. Guanyin became the patron saint of footbinding simply because she was the most beloved deity in the female quarters, always ready to grant the women's secret desires. The lotus also figures prominently in the Guanyin cult. The scripture that bears her name is taken from the *Lotus Sutra* (a sutra is a Buddhist scripture), one of the most popular among female devotees. In another sutra, there is a story about a person being thrown into burning coals but saved by Guanyin, who turned the flames into lotus buds in a lake. In a Chinese devotional story, a general sought the goddess's blessing at the Cave of Tidal Waves, where she is believed to live. Not finding her there, the brutal general shot an arrow into the cave before turning to leave in his boat. All of a sudden lotus flowers sprouted from the water and filled the sea. The general, realizing that Guanyin was nearby, repented and erected a shrine above the cave.[4] The lotus is not only a Buddhist symbol of purity, piety, and wisdom; to devotees of the Guanyin cult it also signifies the apparition of the Goddess of Mercy and her saving grace.

To save people in various kinds of predicaments, Guanyin often appears to people in different forms. In paintings by artists and devotees, one of her earliest poses is that of a Water and Moon Guanyin, holding a willow branch in the right hand and a water bottle in the left. In a tenth-century painting, before Guanyin's sex change, there is an image of him sitting on a rock surrounded by water. Lotus blossoms sprout from the water, and he rests his left foot on one of them. His pose is one of repose (called "royal ease" in art history parlance), and the picture of lotus in water connotes tranquility and peace of mind.

In the most popular image after the sex change, Guanyin appears as the White-Robed Guanyin, an elegant woman wearing a long white cape and often sitting on a lotus throne. In her court female deities of the lotus clan also wear white robes. Not only is white the symbol of purity, like the lotus, but it also symbolizes the mind of the enlightenment, which is the mother of all buddhas and bodhisattvas.[5] By association with whiteness, the lotus also became a complex and somewhat contradictory symbol of purity and motherhood or fertility. When a mother whispered prayers for a pair of properly bound feet to the Bodhisattva Guanyin, she might well be seeking blessings of purity and fertility on her daughter's behalf. Oh the most Compassionate One, she prayed, may lotus blossoms bloom at every step of my daughter's life.

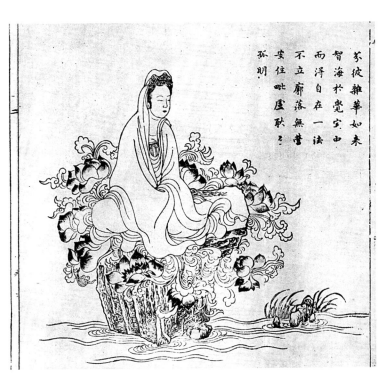

FIGURE 29
The White-Robed Guanyin appears as a young woman sitting on a rock with lotus blossoms sprouting from her seat. One of twenty-eight woodblock prints entitled *The Dabei Dharani of the Bodhisattva Guanyin in Thirty-Two Manifestations* (Guanyin pusa sanshi'er xiang dabei xinqian). Attributed to Ding Yunpeng, ca. 1621–27. From Zhou Wu, *Zhongguo banhua shi tulu*, p. 73, pl. 61.

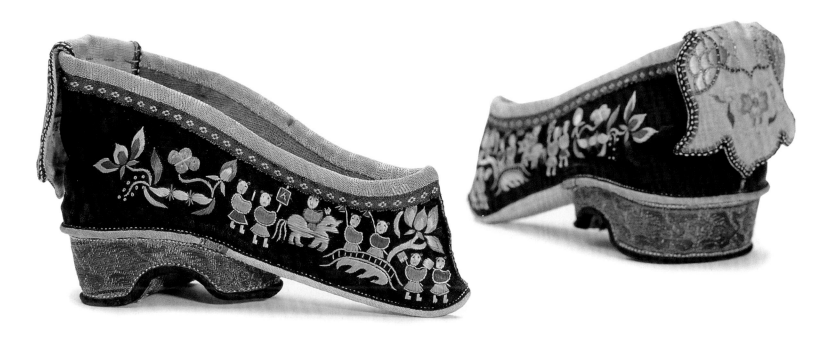

FIGURE 30
Shoes in dark blue satin with
embroidered motif of a successful
examination candidate returning
home on horseback, expressing a
bride's desire for her husband's
career success. Length: 12 cm
(4¾ in.), 20th century. BSM P92.55.AB.

Every Step a Lotus Shoe

On the daughter's footbinding day, she received her first gifts of lotus shoes from her mother. From then on, the mother would teach her one by one all the necessary skills to be a good woman, beginning with sewing and shoe-making. Shoes thus have special emotional meanings to a woman beyond the material aspect. We may say that votive shoes are expressions of her religious devotion, and the first binding shoes are a mother's labor of love. Girls and adult women made shoes as gifts for distant friends and nearby relatives. As a product of a woman's hand, a pair of lotus shoes is not an inanimate object but the material extension of her body and her medium of communication. Literate daughters wrote letters and poetry in their elegant hand, but illiterate daughters spoke through the shoes they made, the shoes they wore, and the shoes they gave away as souvenirs and tokens.

Bridal daughters were literally judged by the shoes they made. Some matchmakers were said to take along a shoe of the prospective bride to show to the groom's family. But the real test came after the betrothal agreement was sealed. A bride-to-be could spend as long as two years making gift shoes for her future in-laws and their entire families. In Zhejiang and other southern provinces, each pair of these shoes would be tied with a bow of colorful silk cord or sewn onto a piece of brocade for presentation. They would then be stored in wooden shoe chests and sent to the groom's family as part of her trousseau, before whom they would be proudly displayed and admired (or harshly criticized.)

The bride-to-be would also lavish attention on her own wedding shoes. Since she was not supposed to loosen her foot binders even for her husband, a pair of soft, socklike sleeping shoes would serve as the focus of his amorous attention. They were often made of red satin, sometimes green, and seldom embroidered save for a tiny flower or baby under the curled tip. Sleeping shoes are perhaps the most tactile of lotus shoes, designed to appeal to the

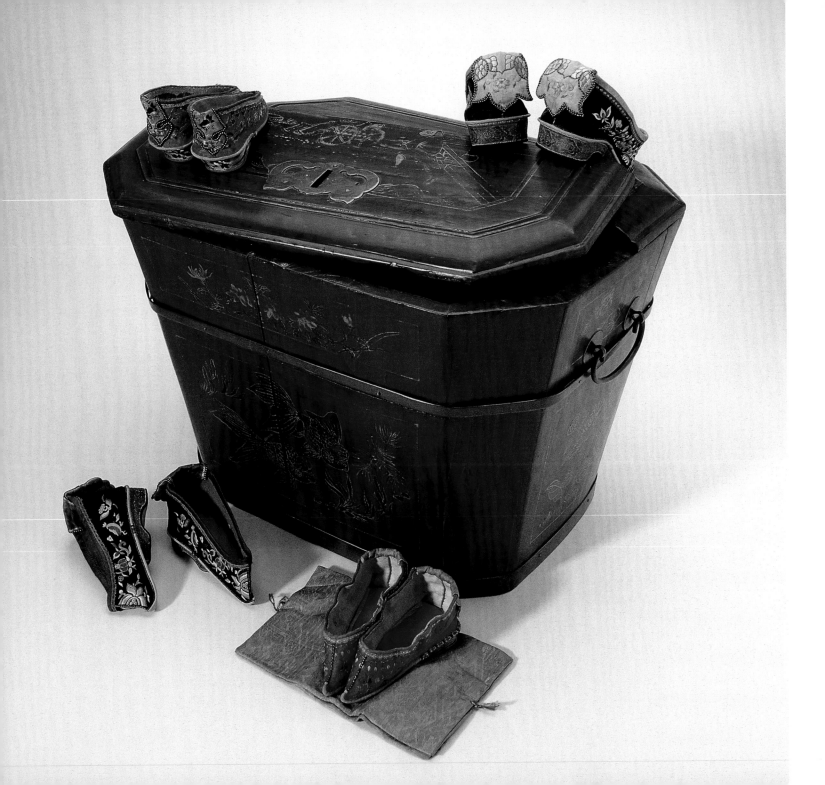

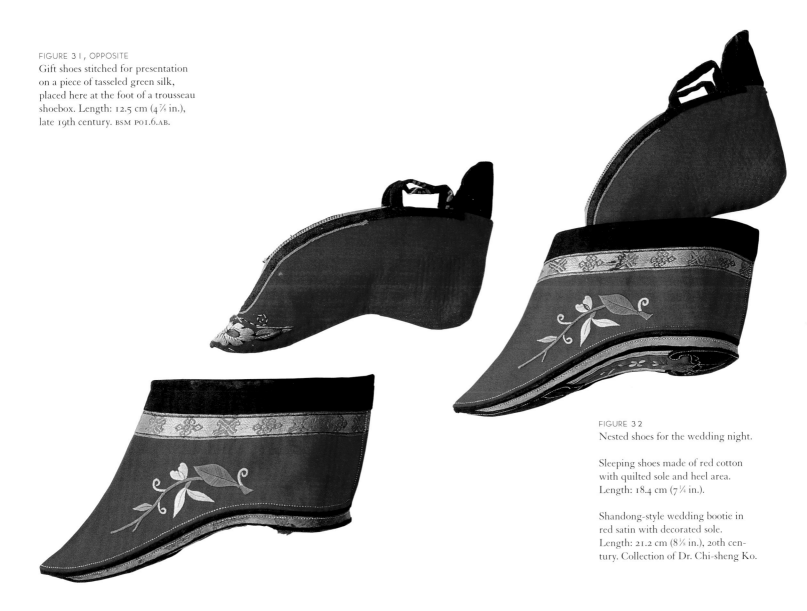

FIGURE 32
Nested shoes for the wedding night.

Sleeping shoes made of red cotton
with quilted sole and heel area.
Length: 18.4 cm (7¼ in.).

Shandong-style wedding bootie in
red satin with decorated sole.
Length: 21.2 cm (8⅜ in.), 20th century. Collection of Dr. Chi-sheng Ko.

sensory experience of touch besides the visual. The sleeping shoe is often the innermost layer in a set of three. Slightly larger would be an indoor shoe with a stiffer sole, to wear inside the bedroom, and finally an outdoor shoe or bootie for a trip to the outhouse. Many women wore sleeping shoes to bed during their entire adult lives. On her wedding night, a bride might have followed a southern custom in handing a pair of sleeping shoes to her groom; "handing over shoes" is a pun for "handing over harmony" (both *xie*). Sleeping shoes also made popular love tokens in the entertainment quarters.

Married women used shoes to express a different kind of love. Although busy with housework and, if they were lucky, child-rearing, brides did not lose contact with their natal families and friends. Those who married far away from home often sent gift shoes to celebrate the birthdays of friends and relatives. Literate women might slip a poem in the shoe, and upon receiving the gift her friend would respond with a poem of her own. One such lucky recipient of gift shoes, a certain Madame Ma, was overjoyed by her friend's thoughtfulness and skills:

> Gratitude for Your Gift Shoes
> *In the azure pond, tiny leaves of golden lotus fall,*
> *Deep in the inner chambers, our happy days of sewing recalled.*
> *Your boundless skills so laboriously sent afar,*
> *Dare I set foot onto the verdant steps, now wet with dew?*[6]

"Azure pond" is the home of the Queen Mother of the West, the most powerful Daoist goddess. Madame Ma paid homage to her friend by comparing her to the goddess. Although the two friends no longer lived in the same vicinity after their respective marriages, a pair of gift shoes reunited them in spirit by recalling the sewing and embroidering they used to do in each other's company as girls.

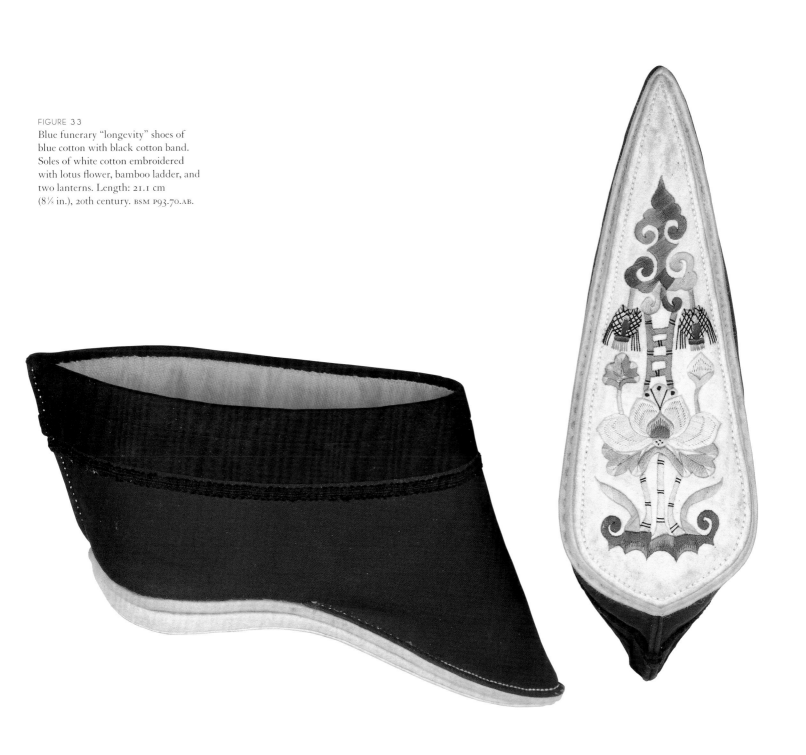

FIGURE 33
Blue funerary "longevity" shoes of
blue cotton with black cotton band.
Soles of white cotton embroidered
with lotus flower, bamboo ladder, and
two lanterns. Length: 21.1 cm
(8⅜ in.), 20th century. BSM P93.70.AB.

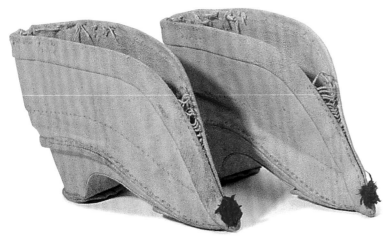

FIGURE 34
Pale mourning shoes of distinct regional styles.

ABOVE
Shanxi-style mourning shoes in pale yellow with purple tuft on tip. Length: 11.1 cm (4⅜ in.), early 20th century. Collection of Douglas D. L. Chong.

RIGHT
Shanxi-style mourning booties. Length: 15.6 cm (6⅛ in.), early 20th century. Collection of Dr. Chi-sheng Ko.

OPPOSITE
Northern-style mourning shoes with white tuft on tip. Length: 15.5 cm (6⅛ in.), early 20th century. Collection of Dr. Chi-sheng Ko.

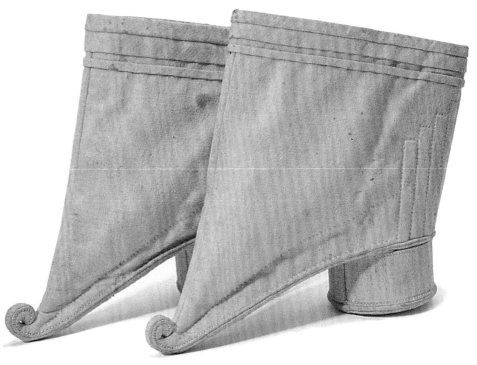

THE FULL CIRCLE

The medical theory that prescribes that a girl comes of age at seven *sui* also suggests that seven cycles later, at age forty-nine, she would cease to menstruate. The end of her fertile years is a cause for celebration for a woman; she has fulfilled her duties to the family as the bearer of sons. She comes full circle when a timid young bride—the bride of her son—presents to her a gift of embroidered shoes. If mothers were loved by their sons, mothers-in-law were to be revered and feared. Such was the bargain a woman struck with the patriarchal family: the pain and tears on her first footbinding day—her ticket to motherhood—finally brought her power and authority within the family when she became a mother-in-law.

Now that someone else was to make the everyday shoes and supervise the kitchen, old women were free to indulge their hearts' desires for the remainder of their lives. Many took religious vows and spent their time embroidering portraits of the Bodhisattva Guanyin. Others entered the most creative period of their artistic careers, spending hours refining their painting brushstrokes or embroidery stitches. There remained one last task of great importance before a woman could relax—making her own funerary (or "longevity") shoes. These shoes are blue with a vamp of plain design; the key message is inscribed on the white sole in the form of a lotus blossom and a ladder or a white crane, her vehicle to the Western Paradise. "Every step a lotus, all the way to heaven"—these would be her last wish for herself. On the day she was laid to rest, her son would slip the shoes on her feet and bid her good-bye with tears in his eyes. Her daughter-in-law retrieved her all-white mourning shoes from the bottom of her wardrobe, tried them on for size, and stepped out of the room knowing that she would be lonelier but not wiser in this world.

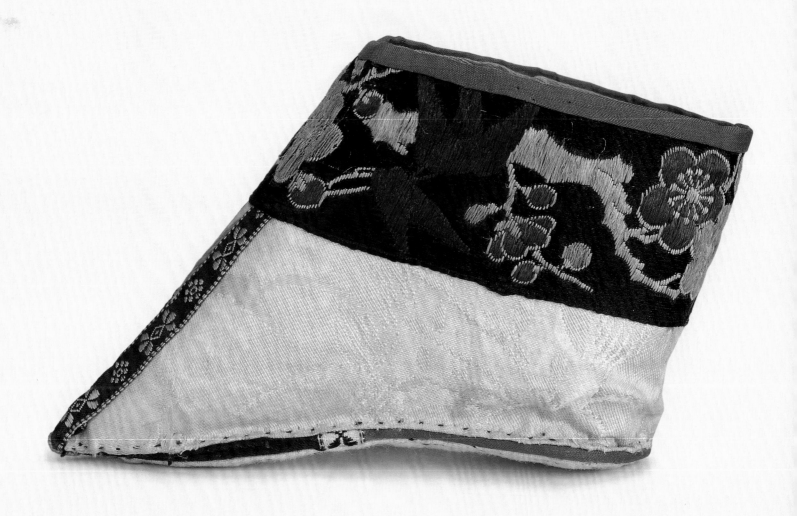

FIGURE 35
Shoe with pink silk vamp and cuff
fashioned from machine-woven
black silk ribbon. Upper stitched to
embroidered cotton sole by hand.
Length: 10 cm (4 in.), early 20th
century. BSM P80.1681.A.

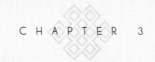

CHAPTER 3

BODIES OF WORK

SHOE-MAKING WAS WOMEN'S WORK, an important skill that mothers taught their daughters. My mother, the daughter of a modest family that operated a porcelain kiln in Hunan, remembers watching her mother making shoes for the whole family. Today, over six decades later, my mother can still recall the process: spreading thick rice paste onto layers of cotton to make soles that were thick and stiff, and then drilling holes into the soles with an awl. My mother, who left home early to attend school, did not learn the skill herself. But even today, in many villages and towns throughout China, women can be seen making shoes—children's animal shoes and adult's kung-fu shoes—stitch by stitch in the old-fashioned way.

A WOMAN'S HAND

Unlike European footwear, which required a wooden last and specialized leather work, traditional Chinese footwear—for men and women alike—was fashioned of silk or cotton and handmade by women of the family. Shoe-making was an essential feminine skill. In fact, shoes were among the most common objects women made—they wore out fast, and both uppers and soles had to be

In ancient times there was a silkworm maiden in the land of Shu whose family name was lost. One day her father was kidnapped, leaving only his stallion at home. She missed her father so much that she made a public promise to the stallion: "I'd marry you if you can bring him back." Hearing these words, the horse galloped to the father's side and in a few days brought him home on its back. When the horse started to wail incessantly, the mother told the father about the promise. He retorted, "A maiden promises herself to a man, not to a horse. How can a human mate an animal? Surely the horse deserves merit in coming to my rescue, but there is no way that the promise can be kept." As the horse started to gallop, the enraged father raised his bow and shot it dead, leaving its skin to dry in the garden. Without warning, the piece of hide leapt off the floor, swept the daughter off her feet, and disappeared with her into the sky. Several days later, the horse's hide was found hanging from a mulberry tree; the maiden, transformed into a silkworm, was nibbling on the leaves. She spun filaments into a cocoon and clothed the world with warmth. One day the maiden, riding the stallion, appeared to her parents in the clouds, and she told them, "The Lord on High has rewarded my righteous heart by making me an immortal consort of the nine skies."

—From Gan Bao, *Soushen ji* (Compendium of the gods)

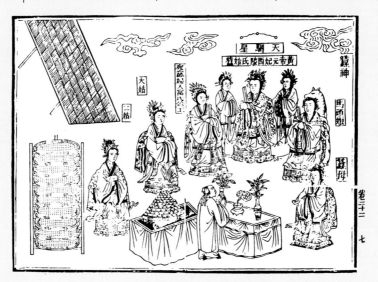

Goddesses of silkworms, including the Horsehead Lady to the right. Seated in the middle is Empress Xiling, the legendary inventor of the silk loom. From Shen Yue, *Nong shu*, ca. 1530, 22: 7ab, reprinted in Dieter Kuhn, *Textile Technology*, p. 261. Courtesy of Cambridge University Press.

constantly repaired or replaced. "Work diligently with your hands" is the charge that Confucian ethics issued to all women, be they young or old, rich or poor. The ideal woman was known not for her beauty or appearance but for her "womanly work" (*nügong*), which could mean mending a sock, sewing a garment, spinning thread, weaving cotton cloth, feeding silkworms, reeling cocoons, embroidering, and shoe-making. Textile work, in all shapes and colors, signaled a woman's moral and economic worth. This is especially true for the lotus shoes she made and wore. "Men plough; women weave" describes the division of labor in an ideal Confucian society.

A bizarre tale first told in a fourth-century collection of stories about folk deities (see "Legend of the Silkworm Maiden") bespeaks the ancient and intimate connection between women and sericulture. From antiquity, the nimble fingers and refined skills required for silk production marked it as genteel women's work. Chinese silk manufacture can be traced to the early Neolithic period, about 5000 BCE. China enjoyed a two-millennium-long monopoly in silk-reeling and weaving technologies since their development more than four thousand years ago. Via the fabled route that came to be known as the Silk Road, silk was exported to lands as far away as Egypt and Rome, where China was known as Serica, the land of silk. It is remarkable that the most highly prized marker of Chinese culture in the Roman world was the product of women's hands.

In the Chinese storybooks, many folk heroines and deities are associated with silk. The silk loom is said to have been invented by Empress Xiling, also called Lei Zu, who was the wife of China's cultural hero, the Yellow Emperor. But it is the Horsehead Lady lore that captures most vividly the intimate link between sericulture and the fecund female body in folk imagination. Until the twentieth century, daughters in silk-producing areas in the Yangzi delta prayed to portraits of the Horsehead Lady for protection of their silkworms, which they called "silk babies." They nursed the worms, just

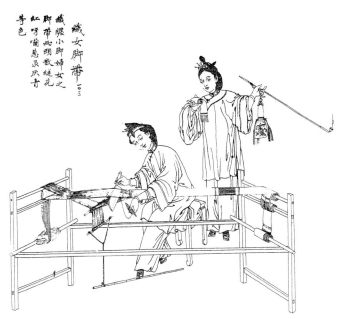

織女脚帶一〇三

藏綣小脚婦女之
脚帶兩頭散縫花
紅呀喘慈泵氏青
等色

FIGURE 36
Women weaving leg sashes with a
hand loom. From a series of prints
brought from China to France by
the Jesuit Père Amiot (1718–93).
Although weaving was a respectable
occupation for women, the purse and
pipe held in the standing woman's
hand suggest that ornamenting the
bound foot was considered frivolous
and wasteful. The caption reads:
"Weaving leg sashes (Zhi nüjiao dai):
Weaving the leg sashes of women
with bound feet. The two ends are
gathered in fringes. In red, blue,
scallion-green, grayish black and
other colors." From Dieter Kuhn,
Die Darstellung, p. 118, fig. 41. Courtesy of the Bibliothèque Nationale de
France.

as they nursed their own babies, by holding them close to
their bosoms. Some people still call silkworms "daughter-
worms." This resemblance between sericulture and motherhood is far reaching. Women's laboring bodies produced
values recognized by society—silk cocoons or children—
and in productive work they realized their own worth.
A good woman worked with her hands and body, for the
benefit of her family and the world at large.[1]

Cotton is an altogether different story. If silk was the
luxury fiber that advertised the wearer's—and maker's—
status, cotton was a pedestrian fiber spun in a peasant's
home. The equipment and skills required for cotton production were simple and accessible. In the eighteenth century, the Qing emperor launched campaigns to promote
cotton planting, spinning, and weaving throughout the
empire with the hope that the morality of the populace
would be renewed by diligent work. If men hoed the land and sowed the
seeds while women spun and wove at home, peasant households would
become self-sufficient and all under heaven would prosper. According to Chinese statecraft philosophy, the industry of the domestic woman was the foundation of public order. Although the goal of self-sufficiency was a utopian
dream, the message for women was clear: the stability and wealth of the
empire depended on the dignity of women's handiwork.

Imperial promotion of cotton production in peasant households fostered a
cult of domesticity for women in the eighteenth century. A loom of her own
enabled a poor daughter to make money for her family without having to
step out of her living room; she could leave field labor to her brothers.
Indeed, it is perhaps no coincidence that footbinding was widely adopted by
women from peasant households and in areas outside the heartland in the

eighteenth century. The downward and outward spread of cotton production allowed these women to claim a symbol of high-class status without having to forgo their economic contributions to the family. In the mid- to late eighteenth century—after the mills in England were operating at full stream—Chinese textile production stacked up favorably against Europe's. Although direct evidence is scarce, it is likely that the spread of cotton technology facilitated the spread of footbinding.[2]

This is the last stage of the meandering journey of the practice of binding feet. It originated one millennium ago among palace dancers and was associated with the decadence of the court. In medieval times, genteel mothers bound their daughters' feet in the inner chambers, where it became a symbol of elite femininity. In each period, the meaning of footbinding and the social location of the women varied. In the eighteenth and early nineteenth centuries, footbinding still carried the aura of an elite practice, but it had quietly undergone a sea change in its social base. The lotus shoe, whether made of refined satin or homespun cotton, continued to be the emblem of such timeless values as status, respectability, and femininity. But the actual social status of its wearer had broadened dramatically at the dawn of the modern period. Since the meaning of binding varies so greatly with time and place, we may think of footbinding not in the singular but in the plural.

SHOE-MAKING

Certain social gradations were reflected in the fabric and construction of the lotus shoes themselves. But the technique for making lotus shoes cut across class and regional differences; the basic techniques for making Chinese footwear—male or female, Han or Manchu—are the same: 1) cutting paper pattern, 2) selecting fabric upper, 3) tracing embroidery design onto fabric, 4) embroidering, 5) affixing lining and finishing the topline, 6) making the sole and heel, 7) stitching upper to bottom, 8) finishing.[3]

FIGURE 37

Shoe-making tools. All date from late nineteenth to early twentieth century, but women have used similar tools for centuries.

Clockwise from top:
Red lacquered wood spool.
BSM P01.34.

Small round bamboo embroidery frame. BSM S01.6.

Awl-like tool in red lacquered wood. BSM P01.14.

Rice paste or glue spreader in red lacquered wood. BSM P01.19.

Lionhead-shaped thread puller in black lacquered wood. BSM P01.21.

Small iron with pointy tip. Collection of Dr. Chi-sheng Ko.

Unpainted wood spool with lotus-shoe-shaped ends. Collection of Dr. Chi-sheng Ko.

Spool in red lacquered wood with drawers for needles. BSM P01.15.

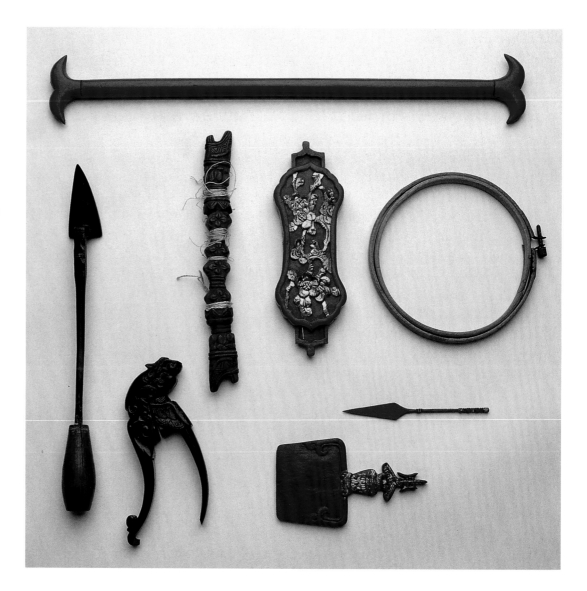

Shoe-making tools were common sewing implements: scissors, needle and thread, bamboo embroidery frame, awl, and small iron. In theory, a pair of lotus shoes that did not have wooden, leather, or metal parts could have been made at home by women's hands alone. This is true for the interior western regions (see chapter 4 for regional styles), where lotus shoes were made of embroidered cotton or consisted of silk uppers with cotton or hemp soles. Soft-soled sleeping slippers from all regions, too, were entirely hand-made, as were the indoor fabric-soled shoes in the southern and northern regions. But outdoor shoes tended to feature wooden heels or soles, which had to be bought or ordered from an outside craftsman—carpentry was men's work. The wooden heels of southern styles were easier to manufacture; they tended to be low and shaped like a coin. In the north, where arched one-piece wooden soles predominated, women went to great lengths to secure skilled carpenters to craft soles for their special-occasion shoes. For daily wear, convenient prefabricated soles of different sizes could be procured from a vendor.

Shoe-making began with the decoration of the uppers. Pattern books showing the outlines of vamp and insole as well as the placement of embroidery designs on them were widely available. In the nineteenth century, shoe designs were sold as part of lithographed pattern books for the seamstress, often alongside patterns for garments and hats. Before the introduction of lithography, shoe patterns were printed by woodblock and appended to household almanacs. Whatever the packaging, shoe designs were readily available to the housebound women because of the vitality of the printing and book trade. These pattern books may be thought of as training manuals or reference books for the women, who would leaf through the pages to learn the rules for selection and spacing of the embroidery designs. They would trace the designs onto another sheet of paper or draw their own, cut them out, and sandwich the individual patterns in between pages of books to keep

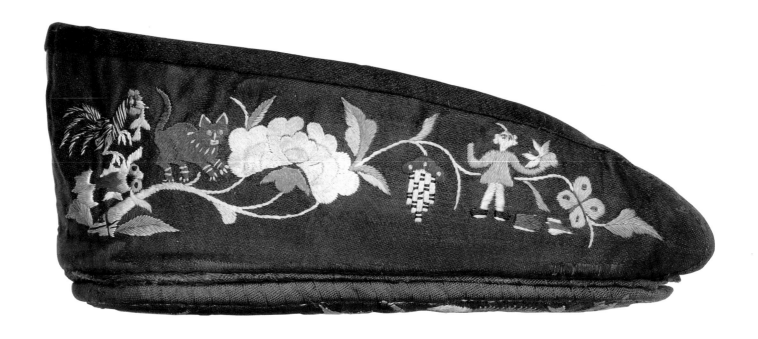
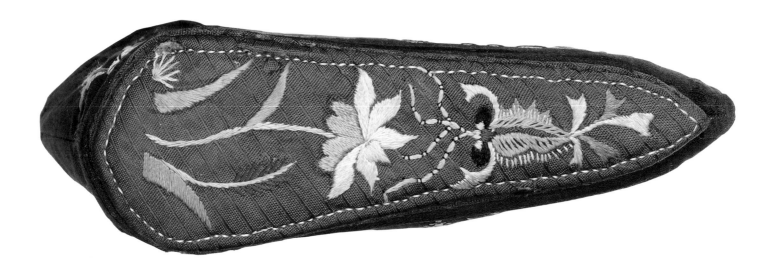

them fresh. The best guides to the aesthetics of shoes were not books, however, but the shoes themselves, which were circulated and admired among friends and relatives in the boudoir.

Once she settled on the design, the shoe-maker decided how to trace the design onto the fabric of her choice: she could stencil the outlines onto the fabric, or tack the entire piece of paper with the stitches outlined on the fabric, which would be embroidered over. She then would be ready to begin embroidering, which is the ultimate test of the shoes'—and the maker's—value. For best results, the fabric for uppers would be stretched on an embroidery frame, stitched, and then cut. Some uppers were first cut and then lined with a piece of cloth or paper, with the raw edges folded in, before they were embroidered. In some cases, such as the uppers of rain shoes made of oiled cloth, the design was painted with a brush instead of embroidered. Appliquéd designs were occasionally used for dramatic color effects, often in conjunction with embroidery stitches.

THE WAY OF EMBROIDERY

Embroidery represents the height of feminine handwork. From altar pieces in temples to portraits and paintings prized in genteel homes, embroidery embellished everyday and art objects alike. Embroidery is both decorative art and "high" art. The most accomplished women were recognized as bona fide artists. Professional needleworkers—poor women and even men—were also capable of turning out sophisticated piece goods ranging from handkerchiefs to theatrical robes with refined stitches. Chinese embroidered goods have been exported to Europe since the sixteenth century, and are found in museums throughout the world today.

The art of embroidery is among the essential skills that mothers transmitted to daughters. A poem written by a sixteenth-century gentry woman, Shen

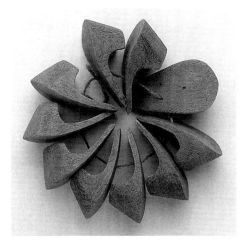

FIGURE 39
String of wooden soles, possibly the ware of a vendor. The arched shape suggests that they were fabricated for northern-style lotus shoes. 20th century. From Ko, Chi-sheng, *Shengui hongyan lei*, p. 61.

FIGURE 38, OPPOSITE
Blue homemade shoes with fabric upper and all-cotton heels. Length: 18 cm (7⅛ in.), 20th century. BSM P00.120.

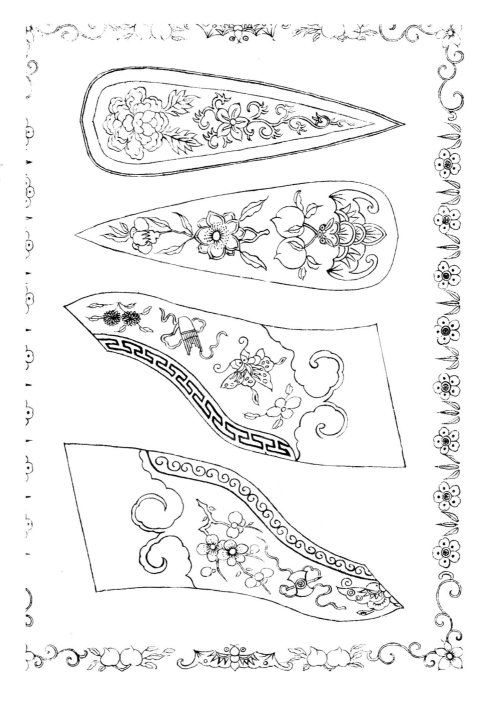

Yixiu, expresses the feelings that overcame her as she, then in her mid-thirties, gave her first embroidery lesson to her teenage daughter:

Teaching Embroidery to My Daughter in Early Summer
Remember at age thirteen,
I first learned embroidery leaning on my bed.
Unaware of the worries that springtime would bring,
I delighted in flowers soon to blossom.
At fifteen I played the flute,
Willow catkins clinging to my sleeves.
Trying a swing with friends,
We frolicked in shadows of grass and flowers.
I started to paint my eyebrows when sixteen,
In springtime I painted them long and slender.
So blows the spring wind for twenty years,
Through long and speechless empty days.
Time flows and renews,
But my morning dreams are the same as ever.
Only that all the roses have wilted,
In this season of sadness.[4]

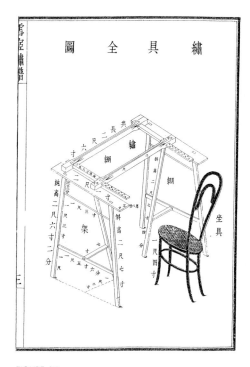

FIGURE 41
Rectangular embroidery frame used by professional embroiderers in the 1910s. The size of each component and the optimal height of the chair are specified in this manual. From Shen Shou, *Xueyi xiu pu*, p. 3a.

"Springtime" and "spring wind" are allusions to sexual awakening in Chinese poetry. Watching her daughter learning to become a woman, Shen Yixiu was swept back in time, to her own coming of age. Embroidery was more than a skill that daughters learned from mothers; it was a conduit for a female culture that one generation of gentry women passed on to the next along with their emotions and dreams.

In the early nineteenth century, a woman artist from the vicinity of Shanghai by the name of Ding Pei decided to share her learning systematically. The result was *The Way of Embroidery (Xiu pu)* published in 1821, the first comprehensive textbook that also contains a systematic aesthetic theory of embroidery. Viewing embroidery as moral cultivation for women on a par with such exalted masculine pursuits as literature and calligraphy, Ding summarized the six essentials of embroidery:

1. finding a quiet, clean, and bright corner as unsullied as the embroiderer's mind;
2. selecting an overall design that is harmonious in the size of the motifs, proportion, and color;
3. choosing the best utensils (silk floss, fabric, scissors, frame, tracing powder) for each task;
4. discerning the subtleties of color gradations;
5. stitching techniques;
6. criteria for artistic appreciation.

For each procedure, Ding gave theoretical and practical guidance. She admonished her readers to practice with seriousness and sincerity, concluding: "The needle is your writing brush; the length of silk your paper; the silk floss your ink. The materials needed are simple but its benefits are numerous. No wonder embroidery is the art of writing for women."[5]

Half a century later, another woman, Shen Shou (1874–1921), won international awards by incorporating into her embroidery the shading techniques employed in oil painting and photography. Ding Pei and Shen Shou developed embroidery as a respectable art. Shen, founder of an embroidery school, also taught the skills as a means of livelihood to commoner women, employed in workshops or at home. After all, there was an enormous demand for shoe uppers, sleeve facings, and garments in the domestic and export market. Preembroidered shoe uppers were widely available as uncut yardage in China in the nineteenth and twentieth centuries, ready to be assembled by the busy women at home.

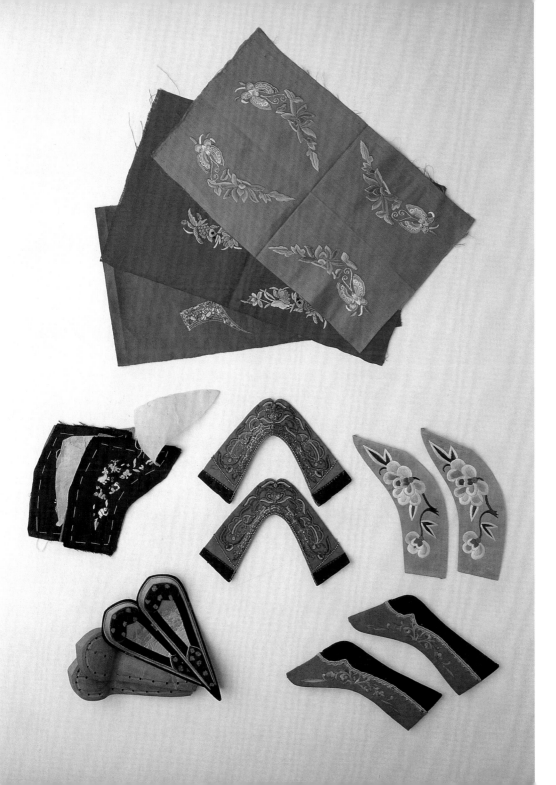

FIGURE 42

Partially finished shoe uppers and soles from the early to mid-twentieth century.

Clockwise from top:
Predecorated uncut shoe uppers. Designs on orange and magenta silk pieces are embroidered, design on brown fabric is painted. Collection of Dr. Chi-sheng Ko.

Turquoise silk uppers. Cut and backed with paper and with raw edges folded down. Collection of Dr. Chi-sheng Ko.

Black and pink silk uppers. BSM S82.0229.AB.

Two pairs of northern-style arched wooden soles, one still bare and the other covered with silk on the side and bottom. Collection of Dr. Chi-sheng Ko.

Cut uppers in black silk with embroidered design protected by tissue paper. Collection of Dr. Chi-sheng Ko.

Pair of embroidered orange silk uppers with heel area trimmed in black and ready to be sewn together. Collection of Vincent V. Comer.

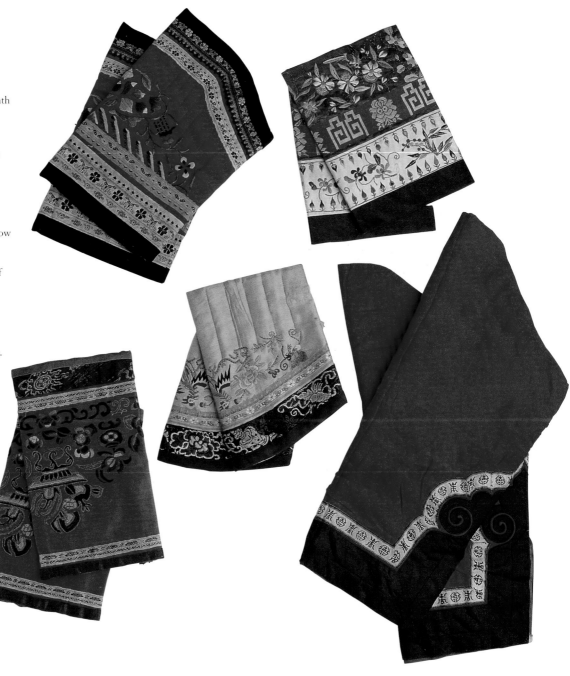

FIGURE 43
Leggings and anklets, late nineteenth to early twentieth century.

Clockwise from upper right: Embroidered anklet trimmed with commercial ribbon. BSM P93.73.AB.

Long legging in red silk with blue trim at the ankle. BSM P01.11.AB.

Padded anklet of embroidered yellow silk. BSM P93.74.AB.

Anklet embroidered with a plate of Buddha's hand fruit. Collection of Dr. Chi-sheng Ko.

Red anklet with embroidery and trimmed with wide ribbon. Collection of Douglas D. L. Chong.

FASHIONING THE SHOES

The majority of lotus shoes are comprised of four uppers—two halves to each shoe. A half-moon or triangular-shaped tongue is sometimes attached to the vamp in southern styles. Before the twentieth century no distinctions were made between the left and right shoe, but the embroidered design sometimes differed for the inward- and outward-facing sides of each shoe. Having been embroidered and cut, the uppers would be lined. In the north, shoes and boots were often lined with felt or padded cotton for the snowy outdoors. The two pieces of uppers for each shoe would then be adjoined at the heel and the tip. For many northern outdoor shoes and boots, a stiff counter made of a roll of thin bamboo strips stitched to a piece of cloth was inserted at the heel. Some women only sewed the tip together, leaving the back seam open so that the exact size of the shoe could be adjusted later.

The last step in the preparation of the upper is finishing the topline and the throat. In some areas, attention was lavished on trimming the topline. In Guangdong, for example, women looped red cords over the edge of the vamp and then wove through the cords with gilt foil to produce intricate geometric patterns (called "damask darning" stitches.) In other areas, a tongue of a different color from the upper was inserted at the throat, and the adjoining area festooned with ribbons or appliquéd cloud-shaped borders. A gusset of crisscrossing thread adorned the throat of some refined southern shoes for decoration and a comfortable fit.

The wooden heel or sole made by a carpenter came with tiny pre-drilled holes for the thread to be drawn. At home, the seamstress began preparation for the bottom by tightly stretching a piece of satin or cloth on the wooden piece. In some areas, the cover fabric was embellished with colorful embroidery, to the point where the bottom of the sole was more ornate than the upper. Top lifts made of cloth (also leather and metal studs in the twentieth century) were affixed on the front and back where the shoe met the ground to prolong the life of the sole. Some outdoor shoes were reinforced with sturdy pegs made of leather, metal, or wood. If stacked cloth soles were used, they would be stitched together with thick stitching to minimize slippage. The needle and thread used were so thick that holes were first drilled with an awl.

The prepared uppers would be stitched onto the sole with needle and thread. Unlike Western footwear, which requires a last that shapes the upper when the shoe-maker secures it to the bottom with tacks, Chinese footwear requires no last or nails. On some shoes a welt of thin white piping was added to the edge where the upper met the bottom. The last step, finishing, varied with style and use. Common elements included tabs on the heel—some were made of coarse cloth to serve as a handle for putting the shoe on; others were made of smooth satin purely for ornamentation. Also attached to the upper during finishing were loops and laces that allowed the shoe to be tied around the ankle. The new pair of lotus shoes was now ready to be tried on.

FASHIONING THE FOOT

A pair of well-made shoes was a key instrument that reshaped a woman's body and allowed her to display it to the world in the most flattering light. Two other items of attire—legging and leg sash—completed the presentation. Like the shoes, these accessories were embroidered and showcased the seamstress's skills. Together with lotus shoes, they covered the flesh, altered the wearer's bodily image, and attracted the viewer's gaze. As such they were articles of fashion and were thus subjected to the vicissitudes of change.

Leggings (*oufu*; *xiku*) are sleevelike lengths of cloth 3 to 4 inches (7.6 to 10.2 cm) wide and up to a foot (30.5 cm) in height. They covered the ankle, often the heels as well, so that only the tip of the lotus shoes peeped out. As early as the sixteenth century, erotic prints showed leggings tied around the ankle with a narrow piece of ribbon, their two ends spreading like a skirt. Together with the shoes, they piqued the viewer's imagination by covering

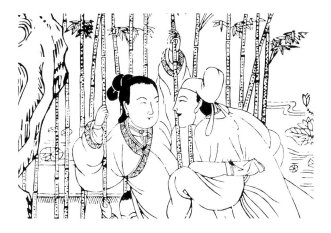

what he most wanted to see but could not. Another accessory is the leg sash (*jiaodai*), a narrow strip of fabric several feet long, used to wrap around the lower part of the leg to define its shape and to enhance support. Before the eighteenth century, the bound feet were always shod even in the most provocative erotic art.

FIGURE 44
Ankletlike leggings tied to the lower calf with ribbons, as shown in Ming erotic prints. *Huaying jinzhen*, nos. 19, 23, in Van Gulik, *Erotic Colour Prints of the Ming Period*, no page.

The size and use of leggings varied with fashion trends and regional differences in the nineteenth and twentieth centuries. In the main, women in northern regions tugged the leg of their pants inside the leggings and tied them with a long sash, accentuating the slenderness of the lower leg. Southern women tended to leave the wide leg of their pants loose. Often instead of a legging underneath, they wrapped their ankle with a long strip of dark-colored cloth. Both methods allowed the wearer to tug in the shoe laces and heel tab for a tidy appearance.

There were endless variations on the legging and sash theme. Some sewed a legging on top of a lotus shoe, turning it into a boot with a beautiful shaft. Toward the last years of the nineteenth century, a new fashion trend developed that favored wearing a tight anklet in between the cloth binder and the shoes. The sock flared slightly at the ankle, which would be tapered with sashes. Just like the shoes, such accessories

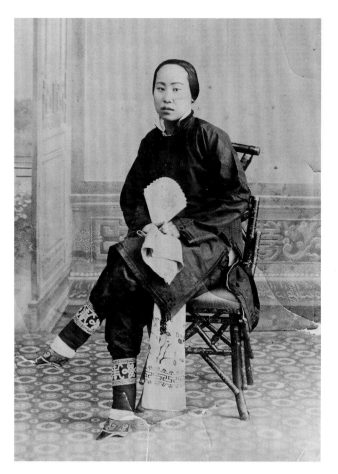

FIGURE 45
Northern woman with the legs of
her pants gathered inside leg sashes
and tight leggings. This style of
dressing draws attention to her lower
leg, especially the bent ankle. Late
Qing period. Courtesy of Dr. Chi-
sheng Ko.

as leggings, anklets, and sashes allowed the wearer to accentuate
certain parts of her lower body, be it the lower calf, ankle, or
arch of the foot. In drawing attention to certain areas of her
body while hiding others, she manipulated the gaze of the
viewer by means of fashion.

A woman would consider herself naked if her feet were not
"tidied up"—first the cloth binder, then the shoe, then the legging or anklet sock, then the sashes, then the leg of her pants,
and then the skirt for formal occasions. It is tempting to conclude that exterior decoration was just as important, if not more
so, than the inner experience of the flesh. The "packaging"—all
products of women's work—was the very source of pride. A
good woman worked with her hands and used her body to display her craft. In the end, isn't the arching of the foot also an
expression of female labor, diligence, and skills?

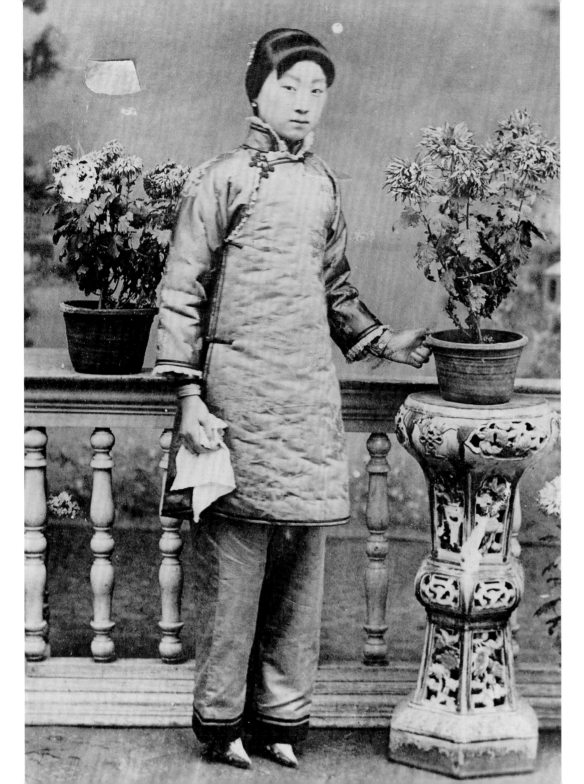

FIGURE 46
Young woman with wide-legged
pants. The thick dark trim calls
attention to the tips of her shoes.
Late Qing, Xuantong period
(1909–1911). Courtesy of Dr. Chi-
sheng Ko.

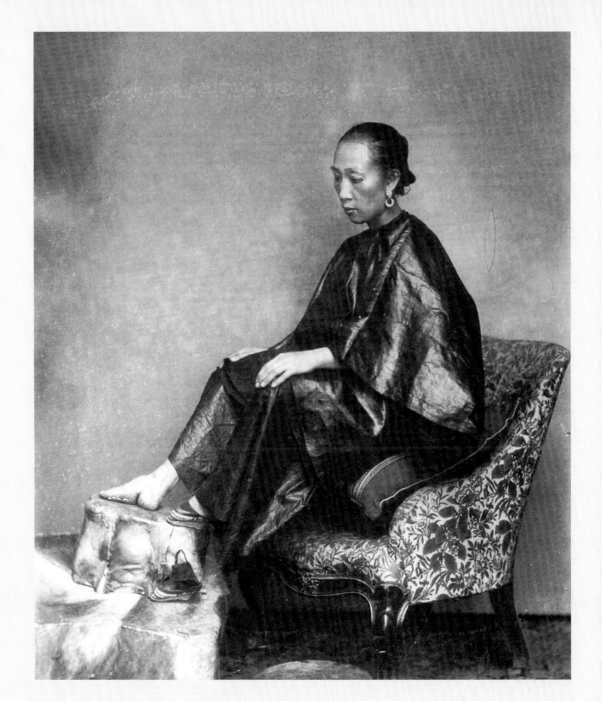

FIGURE 47
*Seated Woman Showing One
Unwrapped Bound Foot*, 1880, albumen print. From Dennis G. Crow
Ltd., *Historic Photographs of Hong
Kong, Canton, and Macao*, p. 57.
Courtesy of Dennis George Crow.

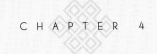

CHAPTER 4

THE SPEAKING SHOE

THE DELICATE STITCHES and ingenious designs on lotus shoes can attain such artistry that they have been collected as art objects since the nineteenth century. The beauty of lotus shoes certainly deserves to be admired, but there is more to the stories they tell. The structure of the shoes, for example, gives clues as to how the shoes physically affected the wearer's body and gait. The style, materials, and artisanship provide a small window into the larger world and historical times in which the shoe was made, worn, and seen. Generals, ministers, and other public figures speak by way of addresses and writings, but the majority of women with bound feet are invisible in history because they did not write. Their lotus shoes speak on their behalf, telling stories about the way these women experienced their bodies, their dreams and hopes, as well as the larger regional and national cultures of which they were a part.

THE BODY

Above all, the shape and structure of the lotus shoe tell us a great deal about how footbinding reshaped a woman's body and altered the image she presented to the world. To appreciate the enormous difference the shoes could make, consider the photograph of a seated woman's feet, the left shod and the right bare. We do not need a caliper to realize that the shod foot *appears* to be inches smaller.

The point here is not that photography is an inaccurate medium, but that the lotus shoes play tricks on our eyes. When we gaze at a pair of lotus shoes in an antique shop or museum, our instinct is to measure its size—the length from tip to heel—and assume that the woman's feet were just as inhumanly small. Four inches, we shudder, that's how much the mutilated girl's feet had shrunk! Without detracting from the strenuous efforts women exerted to make their feet smaller and the pride they felt in their efforts, we should note that most bound feet were in fact bigger than the shoes. The binding cloth manipulated the shape of the foot to conform to a certain shoe style—a gently sloping topline directed the viewer's gaze away from the bulky heel to the pointy toe, for example. In tandem with the binding cloth, the shoes worked like magicians—masters of optical illusion. If successful, the illusion appears so real that the viewer can forget, however momentarily, the annoying fact that everyone inhabits a physical body in a world bound by laws of gravity.

Illusion lay at the heart of footbinding because in anatomical terms, footbinding did not so much destroy the mass of tissues and bones of the foot as redistribute them. This is done in two ways: bending the metatarsal and folding the four digits underneath. In bending the metatarsal into a bulge, binding shortened the distance between the tip of the foot and the heel. The folded digits, in turn, reduced the width of the tip of the foot. The physical effect was a realignment of the ligaments and soft tissues on the foot; generally speaking the result would be a foot with an emaciated arch on top and soft, thick tissues around the crevice on the sole. The length of a shoe is thus no indication of the actual size, or better, "volume" of the foot. Making the feet "small" does not merely mean "short," but involves a complex manipulation of a three-dimensional object in space.

The realignment of the bulk of the foot was achieved primarily by way of the cloth binder. When a woman swaddled her feet with a length of cloth, her overarching objective was not so much to make the feet smaller but to make them *look* smaller. Depending on the region and fashion trend, "smallness" could mean primarily a pointy tip, narrow width, slim arch, or slender ankle. In a perfect world, an ideal pair of bound feet would be distinguished by all of the above, but the majority of women could only hope to accentuate their best feature while hiding the worst. Initial binding bent the arch of a girl's foot, but assiduous maintenance was needed through her life if her feet were to remain well shaped and functional.

To understand how lotus shoes work their magic, let us turn to consider the volume of a shoe. The shoes with the largest volume—space for the bulk of the foot—are northern-style boots with stiff uppers and bamboo-reinforced counters at the heel. With some styles, the shaft of the boot stands straight up, forming a roomy cylindrical case that provides little restriction or support for the top arch of the foot. An aerial view of the sole reveals that although the toe area is slim, the heel area widens considerably. One may imagine the foot of the wearer to be narrow with a pointy big toe, whereas the heel and the arch of the foot could be bulky.

Lotus shoes with a smaller volume than straight-sided booties accommodate the bulk of the foot in other ways. These shoes, mostly southern styles, feature soft uppers and heels without counters. If the booties are display cases for a foot to step into, these low-cut shoes are more akin to scuffs to be stepped onto. Unlike scuffs, however, the fit is tight. The tip of the foot—the big toe—fits snugly into the tip of the shoe, but the arch of the foot is left comfortably alone. The vamp of some styles is so shallow that if not for the loops and laces attached to the topline, which allowed the wearer to strap the shoe on her ankle like a ballerina's slipper, the shoe would not have stayed on her feet. The decorated tip and throat of the front of the shoe provide the

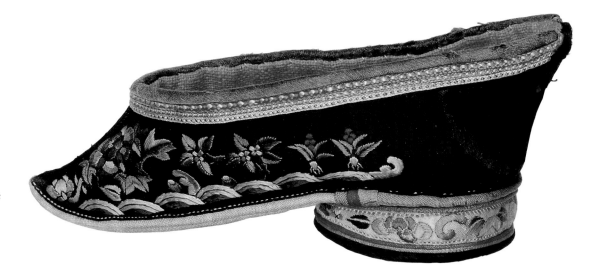

FIGURE 48
Shaoxing-style pumps in dark blue satin. Length: 13 cm (5⅛ in.), 20th century. BSM S92.2.AB.

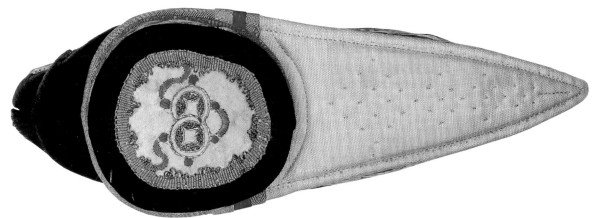

FIGURE 49, OPPOSITE
Shanxi-style booties. Lower half of upper made of embroidered red sil Upper half of black cotton. Quarters stiffened with eight pieces of vertical bamboo boning. Length: 13.5 cm (5⅛ in.), late 19th century. BSM P88.220.AB.

focal point for the viewer's eyes. In the back, hidden under leggings or hemlines of pants and skirts, the heel of the woman's foot could be stepping on the shoe, or hanging outside the shoe. Here, too, the size of the shoe could be much smaller than that of the foot.

Accomplice to the optical illusion wrought by the cloth binder and shoes were "inner heels," coin-shaped wooden blocks that were sometimes attached to the inside of lotus shoes at the heel. The lift elevated the foot at the heel,

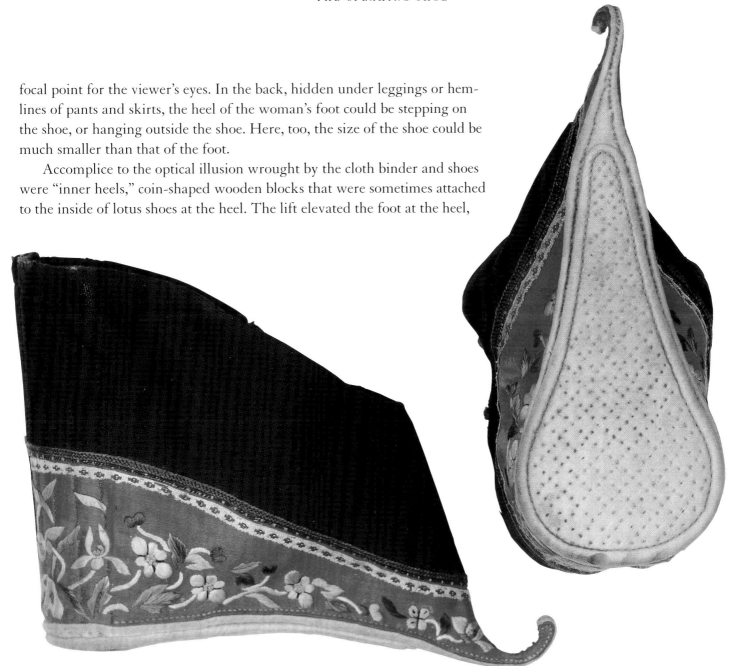

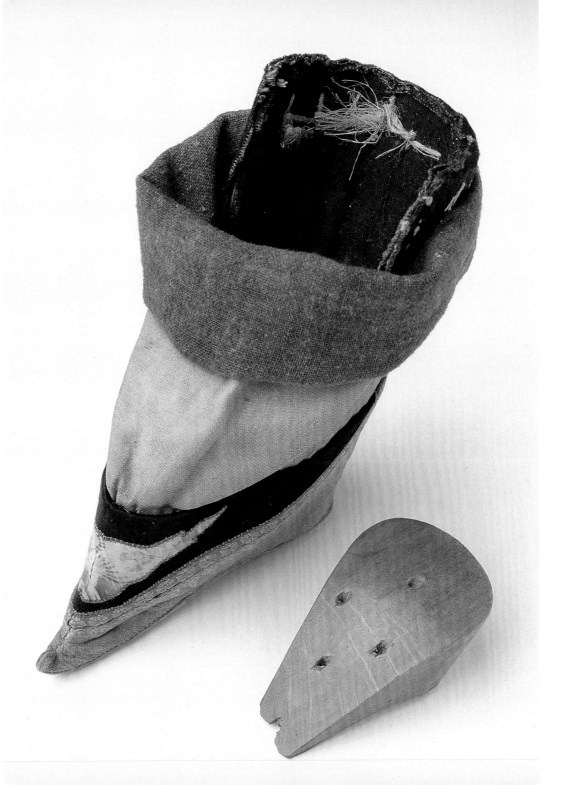

FIGURE 50

The magic of the inner heel. Northern-style boot with cuff folded down, showing bamboo reinforcement extending above the ankle. The triangular "inner heel" fits into the heel area of the shoe, lifting the foot to create the illusion of smallness. Length of shoe: 15.5 cm (6⅛ in.), length of heel: 7 cm (2¾ in.), 20th century. BSM S01.15A.

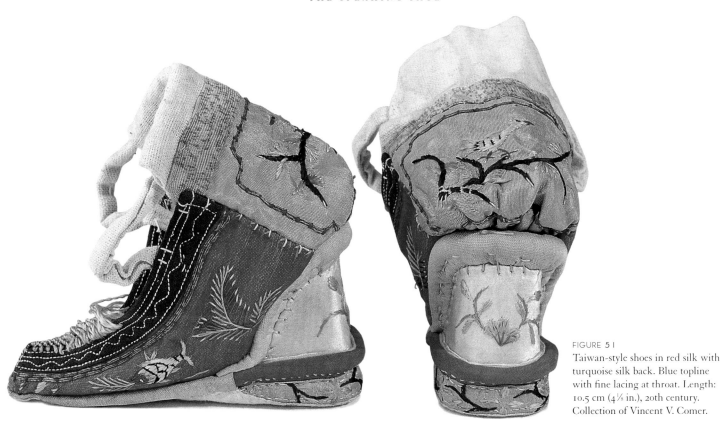

FIGURE 51
Taiwan-style shoes in red silk with
turquoise silk back. Blue topline
with fine lacing at throat. Length:
10.5 cm (4⅛ in.), 20th century.
Collection of Vincent V. Comer.

enabling it to fit into smaller shoes. Some inner heels were so tall that they
allowed the back of the wearer's foot to practically sit outside the shoe.

High-heel lotus shoes served a similar function, with an added advantage
of providing support for walking. A particularly clever design is the Taiwan-
style lotus shoe, which features a sturdy receding high wooden heel and a
bulging back of gathered fabric to accommodate a foot considerably longer
than the shoe. The long back flap hugged the back of the ankle and allowed
the shoe to be secured with laces. The wearer's body weight was distributed
evenly on the padded sole. Affording considerable volume, these are the
sneakers of lotus shoes. The pointy tips, high heels, and bulging back (hidden
under pants) worked together to create the illusion of daintiness.

There is therefore no single answer to the often-asked question: how did footbinding change the bodily movement and gait of a woman? The answer depends on the style of lotus shoes she was wearing. In viewing lotus shoes as instruments of illusion, are we to conclude that the women cheated? In a sense, yes, but it is more accurate to say that "cheating"—displaying the body in the most flattering way—is what footbinding was all about. In their ability to manipulate the viewer's perception, lotus shoes worked in much the same way as items of fashion familiar to us—an empire-waist dress for example.

This view of shoes as items of fashion is neither new nor surprising, but it has an important implication. In a sense, footbinding is more "about" the shoes than the body. We tend to dwell on the flesh and bones when we discuss footbinding—the deformation and pain, which in some ways is a projection of anxieties about our own bodies in our modern society. But in traditional China it was not nature but culture—or shoes as cultural artifacts—that lay at the heart of footbinding's attraction and meaning. The dynamic between the spectacle of the shoe and the flesh concealed is the very dynamic that has generated so much curiosity about footbinding unto the present day.

Visual Puns: Good-Luck Symbols on Shoes

If the shape and volume of lotus shoes give us indirect clues to the modified body hidden under the cloth binders, the design motifs on the shoe uppers and soles tell a different story about the larger world of folk art and folkways of which the shoes were a part. The styles of lotus shoes are shaped by two contradictory forces: as articles of fashion, their style and design change with the wearer and the times. At the same time, the shoe-maker and embroiderer found inspiration from traditional motifs inscribed on temple walls, furniture, altar pieces, garments, and popular prints. These common motifs—bat, fish, golden coins, and others—convey the maker's wishes for the wearer to enjoy fertility, longevity, happiness, wealth, and success.

Of particular interest are good-luck symbols seldom found on objects other than lotus shoes. Most prominent is the symbol of a shoe (*xie*), identical in sound to the word for "harmony." Hence, the motif of a lotus shoe on top of a larger male shoe evokes a scene of conjugal bliss. The symbolism is subtle, but the erotic connotation is unmistakable.

On the margins of literary discourses, the world of Chinese folk art and popular religion is rich in symbolic meanings. Pictures of a lotus flower or a bat say a lot—both maker and wearer recognize immediately what they

FIGURE 52
Red silk shoes with an embroidered motif of one female shoe floating on top of a larger male shoe. Double coin motif on bottom of the heel. Length: 11.5 cm (4½ in.), 20th century. BSM P92.3AB.

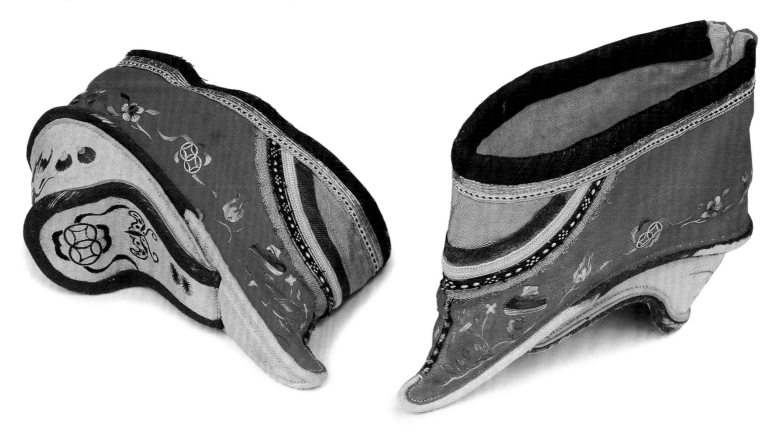

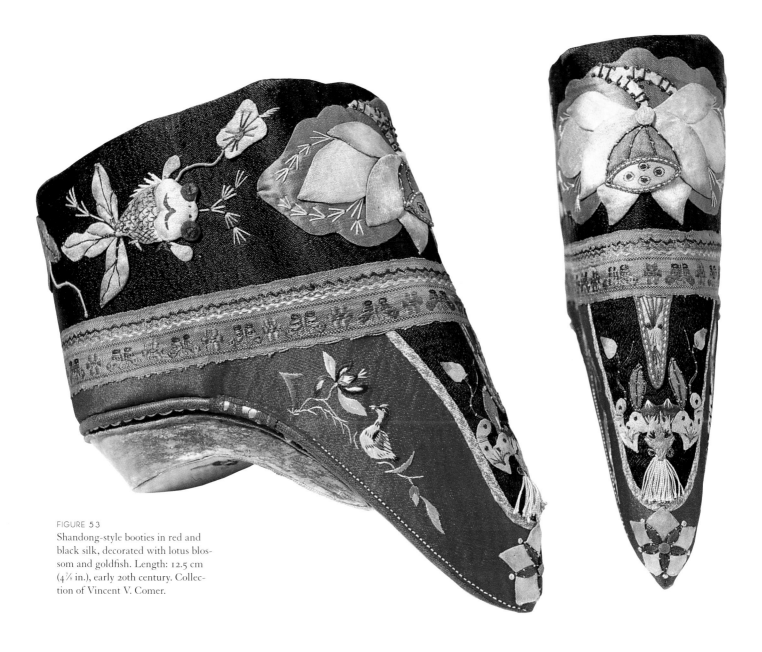

FIGURE 53
Shandong-style booties in red and
black silk, decorated with lotus blossom and goldfish. Length: 12.5 cm
(4⅞ in.), early 20th century. Collection of Vincent V. Comer.

stand for—without the need for the written word. There are three common ways of linking symbol to meaning: direct indication, visual pun, and narrative. Direct indication works by simply drawing the objects desired. Fertility is expressed by a string of children or a pomegranate bursting open with seeds; a turtle signals longevity. An abstract symbol could also indicate meaning in this straightforward way; a prime example is the swastika, which is a Buddhist symbol of good luck widely used in Asia.

Visual punning is pervasive in Chinese culture because the Chinese language, being monosyllabic, has a limited repertoire of sounds—about four hundred. Each sound (*xie* for example) corresponds to a multitude of written forms that mean vastly different things: shoes, harmony, to rest, to write, tilted, and many more. An abstract quality such as harmony can thus be depicted pictorially with a concrete object in the form of a shoe (see "Visual Puns on Lotus Shoes").

Visual puns and shared symbols such as the swastika allow the majority of the Chinese—illiterate men, women, and children—to create and convey meanings without using the written language. The symbols on the lotus shoes bespeak personal and collective wishes for a better life. Even more important to the everyday and emotional lives of the women with bound feet were legends populated by feisty deities, caring goddesses, heroic knights-errant, or monstrous beasts. Attributes of these characters and the plots in which they appear were circulated from village to village by itinerant storytellers and operatic troupes. Year after year and century after century these elements collected in popular memory as a cultural currency understood by all. Hence, when someone saw these elements embroidered on a lotus shoe, the entire story or legend and its pathos would be conjured.

The Eight Immortals, a colorful group of Daoist holy men and women, supply many of the good-luck symbols in popular culture, as on lotus shoes. Among them is He Xiangu, daughter of a shopkeeper who became an

VISUAL PUNS ON LOTUS SHOES

Bat: happiness (*fu*)
Shoes: harmony (*xie*)
Fish: surplus (*yu*)
Lotus: continuous (*lian*)

Entire phrases or sentences can be composed using visual puns:

Lotus (*lian*), mouth organ (*sheng*), precious (*gui*),
sons/children (*zi*)

Continuous (*lian*), give birth to (*sheng*), precious (*gui*),
sons/children (*zi*)

Lotus (*lian*), fish (*yu*)

Continuous (*lian*), surplus (*yu*)

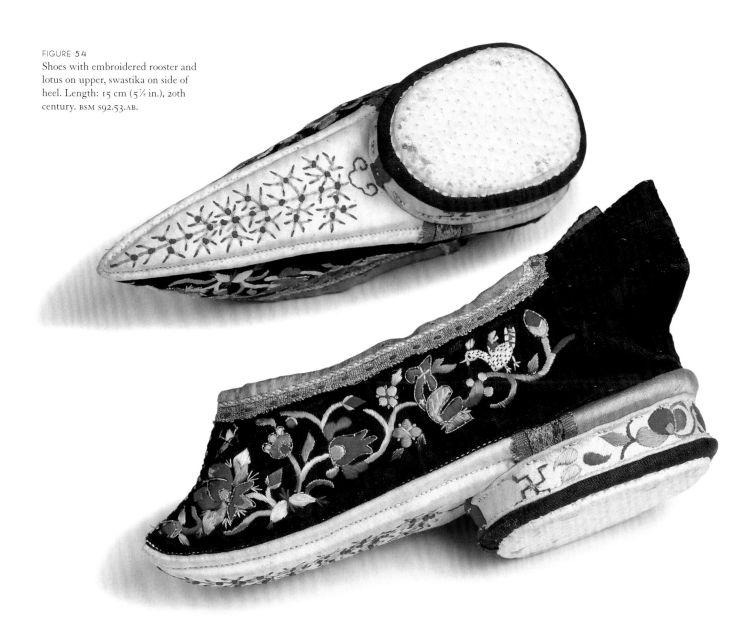

FIGURE 54
Shoes with embroidered rooster and lotus on upper, swastika on side of heel. Length: 15 cm (5⅞ in.), 20th century. BSM S92.53.AB.

immortal upon eating a peach. She carries a stem of lotus in her hand. Another immortal, Lan Caihe, is always depicted with a basketful of flowers. The personal emblems of the other six include a fan, sword, gourd, pair of castanets, flute, and bamboo cane. Another Daoist holy man whose attributes are found on lotus shoes is Liu Hai, who appears in folklore with a three-legged toad, a dweller of the Moon and a symbol of the unattainable. When the toad escapes into a well, Liu would fish it out with a string of coins. Hence, both the coins and the three-legged toad are considered harbingers of good fortune and wealth.

In searching for the meanings behind the symbols found on lotus shoes, we come to appreciate how the shoes draw from, and are an integral part of, Chinese folk culture and mores. In using this shared set of visual vocabulary, the shoe-maker expressed and conveyed deeply felt sentiments such as the wish for children and wealth. There is a danger, however, in overreading the symbols or in assuming that every sign on the vamp must have profound meaning. This is not the case. A great number of lotus shoes are decorated with generic floral motifs or swirling cloud patterns. Often the meaning of a shoe and the story it bespeaks do not lie in its design motif but in its social life—how it was given away, sold, worn, repaired, and how it was viewed at the time. Unfortunately, details about the use and consumption of particular lotus shoes disappeared with the passing of the women who made or wore them. All that we can know with some certainty is the reception and perception of lotus shoes as a group.

REGIONAL CULTURES

Classified by shape, composition, and construction, lotus shoes yield a wealth of information on regional cultures in China. The distinct shoe styles from each region tell stories about its diverse ways of life.

Major regional styles of lotus shoes

Footbinding became so popular in the eighteenth and nineteenth centuries that each region in China developed its own style of lotus shoes. In their divergent shapes and styles, lotus shoes express the diversity of local cultures. This map highlights the cores of regions where some of the most distinctive styles of lotus shoes originated (areas shown are approximate).

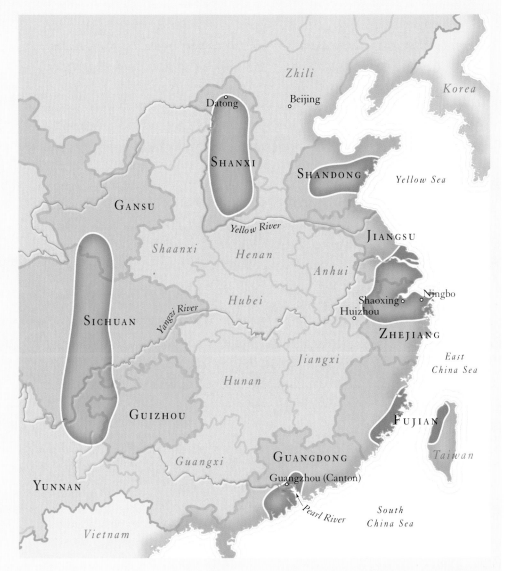

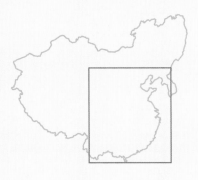

In the north, where the landscape is defined by dry fields planted with sorghum, millet, and wheat, booties with stiff uppers, arched wooden soles, and bamboo-strip counters were often worn on top of soft-soled sleeping or indoor slippers. These booties were display cases, often with ornate soles. This may have something to do with the fact that in the bitterly cold northern winters, the most efficient way to keep everybody in the house warm is a large heated platform bed (*kang*) adjacent to the stove. At night the family huddles on it; in the daytime women perform many daily chores sitting on it, from sewing to cooking. The beautiful soles decorated with elaborate embroidery and patchwork could be showcased at eye level. The cold weather also explains why many northern shoes are padded with cotton or silk and, later in the twentieth century, made of felt.

The two main groups of northern regional styles—northeast (Shandong province, also neighboring Hebei) and northwest (Shanxi province)—include a large repertoire of shoes and boots marked by creative designs and sophisticated workmanship.

If climatic or ecological factors help explain some of the broad differences between northern and southern styles, local economic factors are important in determining the materials and techniques used in the making of a particular pair of shoes. Here, instead of north-south differences, let us examine regional variations. In Taiwan and the vast interior regions, uppers and soles made of homespun cotton predominated. We may surmise from the fabric and stitching that women made these shoes by hand using locally available materials, without professional help or imported materials. In other words, these lotus shoes were products of the domestic economy.

In areas more affected by trade, the lotus shoes women made tended to include purchased parts—wooden heels, fine silk floss, machine-woven ribbons and laces, or the silk uppers themselves. Given the advanced state of the Chinese economy in the nineteenth century, no region was left untouched by

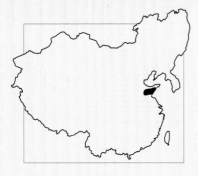

FIGURE 55

Shandong Region

Footbinding was so popular on this northern peninsula that even poor women who worked in the fields had bound feet.

Shandong shoes are distinguished by their ornate soles, sometimes with kidney-shaped heels.

Shandong booties feature a downward toe and a straight shaft. Both shoes and booties feature a wooden sole covered in fabric.

SHANDONG SHOES

- Ornate sole
- Curved wooden sole covered with fabric

SHANDONG BOOTIES

- Wide shaft; almost vertical wall
- Toe area arched downward

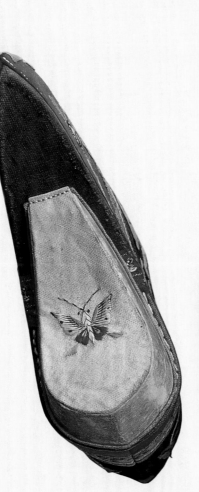
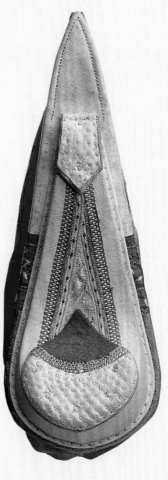
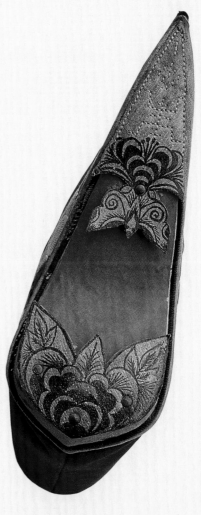

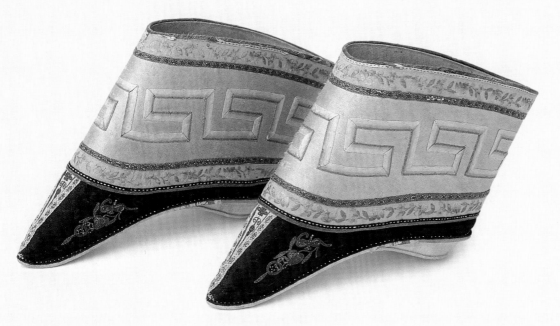

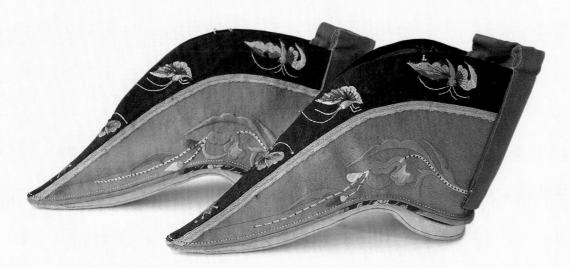

FIGURE 56, OPPOSITE
Decorated soles of Shandong-style shoes from the early twentieth century.

Left to right:
Heel covered with white cotton with embroidered butterfly. Length: 12.5 cm (4⅞ in.). Collection of Vincent V. Comer.

Curved cotton-covered sole with silk ribbon appliqué. Tear-shaped top lift of quilted white and magenta cotton. Length: 14 cm (5½ in.). BSM P79.0512.A.

Sole covered in pale magenta fabric with leather top lifts. Floral and butterfly designs drawn on leather with ink. Length: 15 cm (5⅞ in.). Collection of Dr. Chi-sheng Ko.

FIGURE 57, LEFT
Stiff dark blue and gray satin Shandong-style booties. V-shaped insert at toe embroidered in gold thread. Cuff wrought of three-tone blue ribbon on gray satin with Roman key design. Length: 18.6 cm (7⅜ in.), late 19th century. BSM P86.0011.AB.

FIGURE 58, BELOW
Shandong-style shoes in pink silk with arched wooden sole covered in white cotton. Length: 18.5 cm (7¼ in.), 20th century. Collection of Vincent V. Comer.

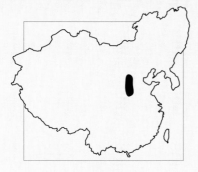

FIGURE 59

Shanxi Region

O n this northern dry plateau by the banks of the majestic Yellow River, women developed many distinct local styles of lotus shoes. Three representative types are:

FIGURE 60
Datong-style high-heeled shoes with fine lacing. Upper in ivory fabric decorated with thick topline in geometric pattern. Length: 8 cm (3⅛ in.), late 19th century. BSM P82.32.AB.

JIN STYLE

· Flat sole
· Bamboo reinforced counter
· Embroidered decoration along bottom of the upper
· Sometimes a curled toe

SHOES WITH DRUM-SHAPED HEELS

· Low and round drum-shaped heel
· Extremely narrow sole at the arch and toe area

DATONG CITY STYLE

Datong City in Shanxi was renowned for the design and artisanship of lotus shoes. Among its distinctive designs is one characterized by a gently curved one-piece wooden sole and a sloping border on the vamp that directs the viewer's eye to the tip of the toe.

· Curved one-piece wooden sole covered with fabric
· Sloping topline on vamp

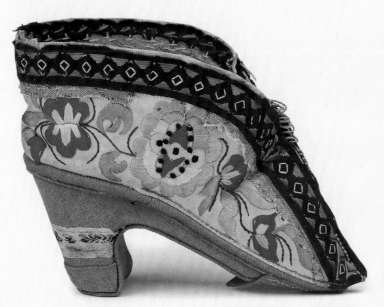

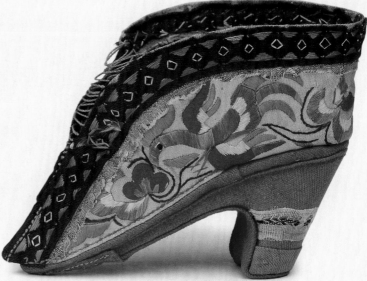

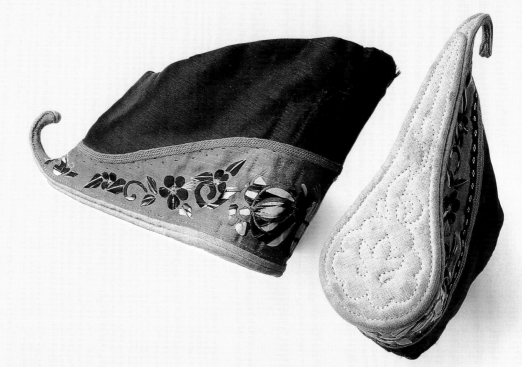

FIGURE 61, RIGHT
Jin-style booties with curled toes. Lower half made of embroidered pale blue silk. Heel area reinforced with strips of cotton-covered bamboo. Length: 14.5 cm (5¾ in.), 20th century. Collection of Dr. Chi-sheng Ko.

FIGURE 62, BELOW
Shoes with curled toes in red satin. Multicolored embroidered vamp edged with black topline. Cylindrical heel covered with commercial ribbon. Length: 17 cm (6¾ in.), 20th century. Collection of Dr. Chi-sheng Ko.

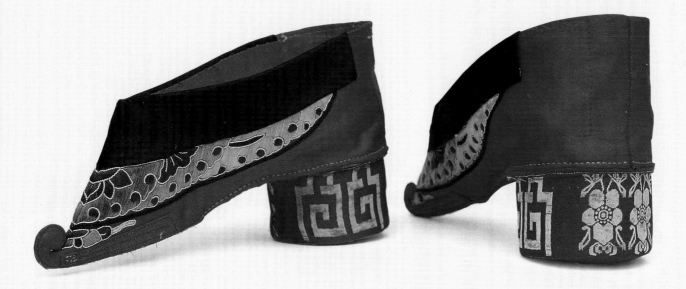

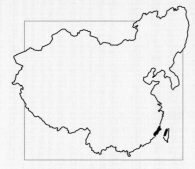

FIGURE 63

Fujian and Taiwan Regions

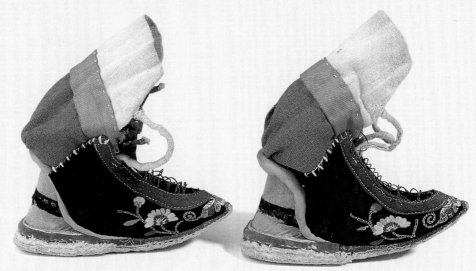

Settlers from Fujian province brought their style of lotus shoes to Taiwan. These shoes feature a very high heel and a gathered fabric back that curves sharply forward, allowing the shoe to be much smaller than the length of the wearer's foot. Many of the shoes from this region are made of cotton, not silk.

FUJIAN AND TAIWAN SHOES

· High wedge heel
· Gathered, bulging fabric back

FIGURE 64
Taiwan-style shoes in dark blue cotton. Gathered heel area in green and pink cotton. Length: 13.2 cm (5⅛ in.), 20th century. BSM s82.0129.AB.

FIGURE 65
Taiwan-style shoes in dark blue cotton. Gathered heel area in red and pink cotton. Length: 15.2 cm (6 in.), 20th century. BSM s82.0131.AB.

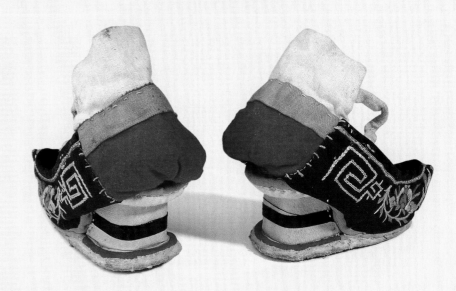

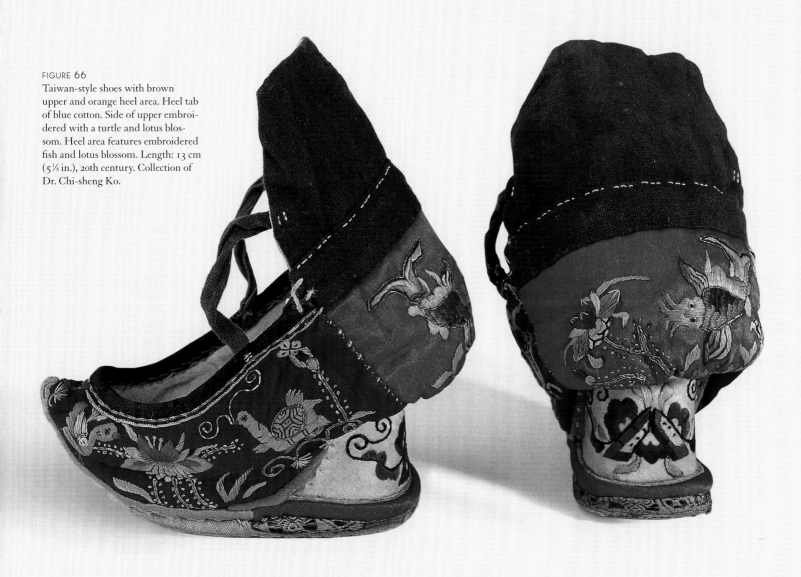

FIGURE 66
Taiwan-style shoes with brown
upper and orange heel area. Heel tab
of blue cotton. Side of upper embroidered with a turtle and lotus blossom. Heel area features embroidered
fish and lotus blossom. Length: 13 cm
(5⅛ in.), 20th century. Collection of
Dr. Chi-sheng Ko.

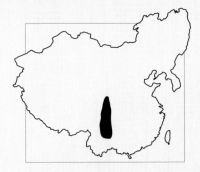

FIGURE 67

Interior Northwest and Southwest Region

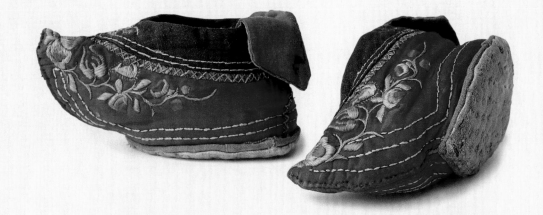

Footbinding came late to the vast regions of the interior, often a result of Han Chinese settlers moving into frontier areas populated by ethnic minority groups.

Shoes from these areas, sometimes called "minority shoes," are less complicated in design and construction. Seldom made of silk, they feature simple embroidery on homespun cotton and flat soles of stacked cotton.

INTERIOR NORTHWEST AND SOUTHWEST SHOES

- Cotton upper
- Simple construction
- Flat sole
- Often with upturned nose

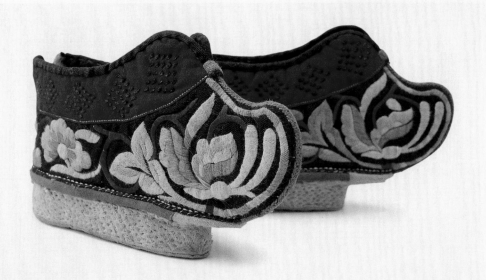

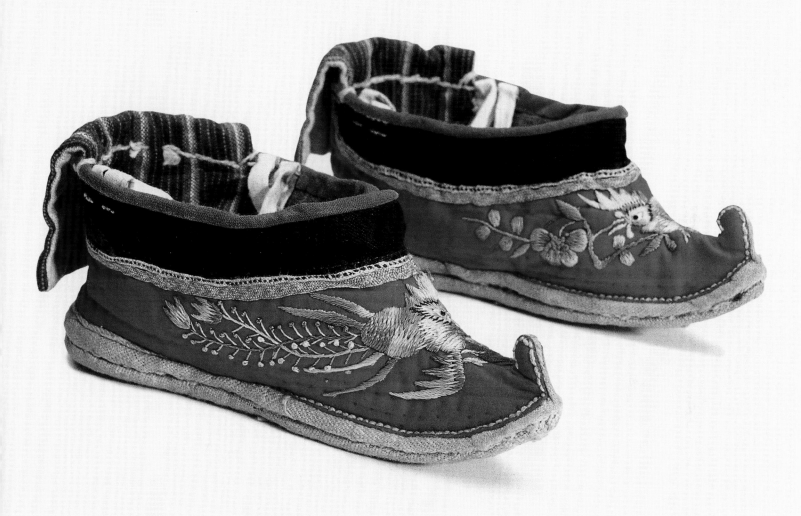

FIGURE 68, OPPOSITE, ABOVE
Red silk shoes from Sichuan province
with overhanging toes. Sole made of
stitched cotton. Length: 15 cm (5⅞ in.),
20th century. Collection of Dr.
Chi-sheng Ko.

FIGURE 69, OPPOSITE, BELOW
Embroidered shoes from the Qinghai
area in blue cotton with brown topline
decorated with geometric patterns.
Overhanging upturned toes with multi-
layer cotton sole. Length: 18.2 cm
(7⅛ in.). Collection of Dr. Chi-sheng Ko.

FIGURE 70, ABOVE
Shoes in red cotton with layered cotton
sole. Topline of dark blue cotton edged
with light blue cotton. Length: 16.3 cm
(6⅜ in.), 20th century. Collection of
Dr. Chi-sheng Ko.

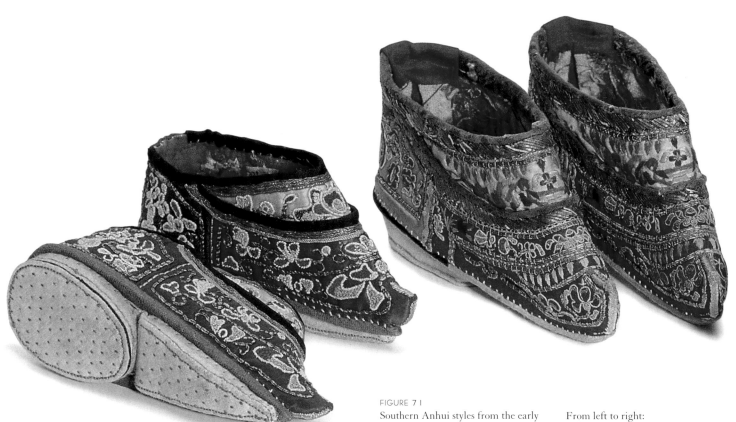

Southern Anhui styles from the early twentieth century. All uppers made of cotton covered with multicolored embroidery. Characteristics of the style are the arc at the throat in contrasting color, uppers covered with decoration, and frequent use of French knot stitches and gold couching.

From left to right:
Length: 13 cm (5⅛ in.).
BSM P01.25.AB.

Length: 15.5 cm (6⅛ in.).
BSM P01.23.AB.

OPPOSITE
Length: 13.5 cm (5⅛ in.).
BSM P01.26.AB.

the crisscrossing marketing networks. A majority of the lotus shoes were made of components produced at the crossroads of the domestic economy and the commercial economy. A woman could stitch her hand-embroidered upper to a purchased sole, or she would embroider the uppers herself and ask a hired seamstress to finish the rest. The exact proportion of the two varied from area to area and from shoe to shoe. If we analyze the "foreign" element of each shoe—imported chemical dyes, machine-woven laces, or machine stitching—we may find valuable clues to not only the workmanship but also the dating of the shoes.

Although climatic and economic conditions play a part, ultimately it is subjective tastes and local artistic traditions that are most salient in determining how a lotus shoe looks and feels. Some regional distinctions are subtle and discernible only to local eyes, but the lotus shoes from some locales developed such strong visual characteristics that they are landmarks of their places of origin. One example is Yi county, part of Huizhou prefecture in Anhui province. Home of the famed Huizhou merchants active in the lucrative salt and lumber trade in the Qing dynasty, this area was enriched by the profits these merchants sent home. The majestic temples and ancestral shrines dotting the landscape were products of a cosmopolitan mixing of styles that the merchants brought home from all over the empire. So, too, were the lotus shoes. The distinct look of Huizhou shoes derives from the all-over embroidery on the upper using a variety of stitches—especially French knots—which highlights the tactile texture. Fancy gold couching is common. The two-part sole and heel are usually flat, not

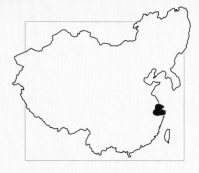

Jiangsu and Zhejiang Region

FIGURE 72

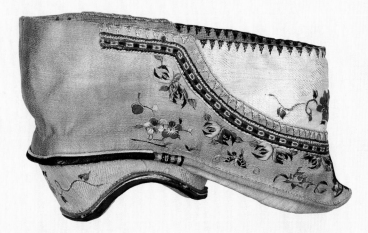

This southern heartland was the center of the Chinese silk and cotton industries. In general, southern shoes have softer vamps and lower heels. The heels are made of either wood or cotton textiles. Unlike the one-piece northern wooden soles, southern soles are more flexible, made of two separate pieces stitched onto a fabric innersole. Two representative types are:

LADDER-RUNG SHOES

Ladder-rung shoes exemplify the elegant southern style. They feature elongated uppers in unusual pale colors, often pastel or white, and delicate "ladder rung" lacing.

- Fine elongated lacing
- Upper of pastel-colored satin
- Upper with soft walls

SHOES FROM NINGBO AND SHAOXING

These shoes often resemble Western low-heeled pumps. Also common are shoes with apronlike tongues and gentle concave heels.

- Intricate all-over embroidery on upper
- Low heel, often decorated
- Front of sole and heel in separate pieces
- Some with semicircular insert above toe

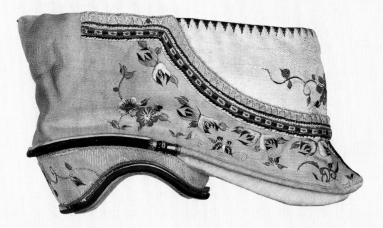

FIGURE 73
Pale blue silk shoes with white damask insert above the toes, edged with commercial ribbon. Length: 12 cm (4¾ in.), 1870–1900. BSM P96.104.AB.

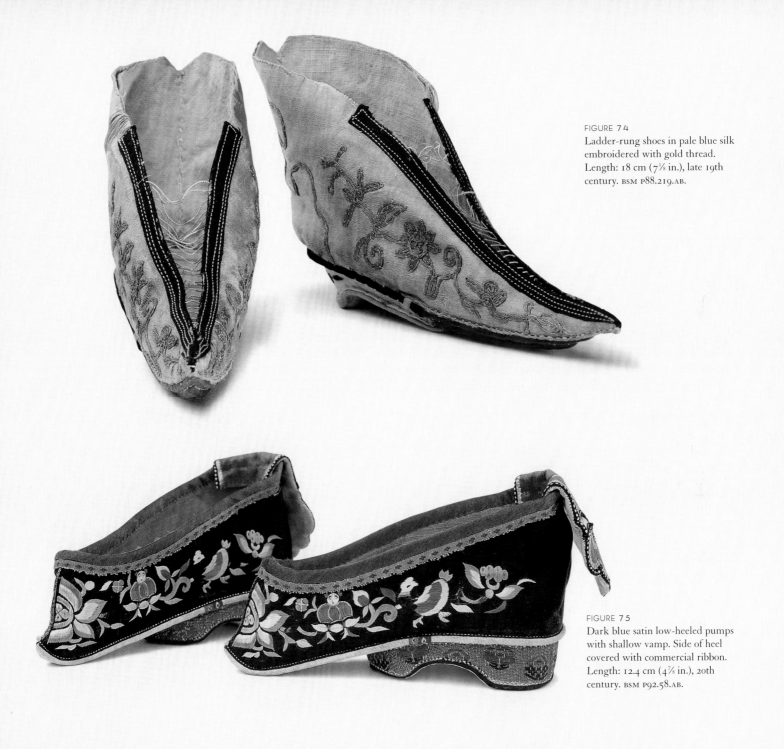

FIGURE 74
Ladder-rung shoes in pale blue silk embroidered with gold thread. Length: 18 cm (7⅛ in.), late 19th century. BSM P88.219.AB.

FIGURE 75
Dark blue satin low-heeled pumps with shallow vamp. Side of heel covered with commercial ribbon. Length: 12.4 cm (4⅞ in.), 20th century. BSM P92.58.AB.

THE CANTONESE LOTUS SHOES DEFINED

by Douglas D. L. Chong

One of the most diminutive styles of lotus shoes was the classic Cantonese slippers worn by women from the Pearl River delta region of Guangdong Province. This geographic area included Canton City [Guangzhou] in the north, Sanyi (Sam Yup) and Zhongshan (Chung Shan) counties in the middle, the Siyi (See Yup) region to the west and Hong Kong in the southeast. Most of the Chinese women who migrated to America during the nineteenth and early-twentieth centuries came from this region.

Various characteristics of the Cantonese shoe distinguished it from styles of the north. One key structural feature was the extremely tiny appearance of the shoe effected by a low vamp, high wedge heel, and the lack of an extended sloping toe present in northern shoes. The wall of the shoe rose straight up at a vertical angle, much like the old Shanxi boots. To create a dainty and elegant point that sometimes peeked underneath a long skirt, the toe was slightly upturned and the tip was sometimes embellished with a tiny pearl or jade bead.

The body of the shoe was made of fine silk, thick satin, or brocade. Most distinctive was a thick woven band lining the top of the vamp, created by looping thick red cords over the top of the shoe and weaving it through a layer of gilt foil in the front to create an intricate geometric pattern. These patterns, designed by the women themselves, were highly guarded as individual creations, for no two designs were the same. All celebratory, votive, and dressy shoes were decorated with this unique band which was sometimes made in pink, turquoise, purple, or black. For everyday wear, the topline was lined with a solid band of fabric, with or without embroidered emblems.

The sides of the shoes were decorated with designs favored by the Cantonese—lotus, butterflies, peach blossoms and chickens. Variations also included the curling cloud, lotus, vines with leaves, "bak lan" flowers, peony, pomegranate, double coins, endless knot, and the phoenix. The front toe was embellished with either of two primary symbols, a stylized lotus or a butterfly. Designs on the shoe were either couched with silver and gold threads or satin stitched with fine silken floss. A unique looping chain stitch of gold thread frequently sectioned off the frontal design of the shoe.

The back ends of the shoe did not meet and therefore were never stitched together, as they were in other lotus shoes. Instead, the side walls were kept short of the back heel area, creating an open back. This opening later accommodated an added heel strap that extended high above the shoe and served as a heel lift or heel strap. The heel strap, made of rough black linen, blue cotton, or white linen, was stitched to the shoe walls. The function of the heel strap was twofold: to accommodate the proper size of the wearer's heel and to secure the shoe to the foot. Two separate loops attached the strap to the side walls of the shoe. These heel lift reinforcements, or functional loops allowed the woman to tie and secure the shoe to the foot.

After the uppers were made, the shoe was finally fitted with a high wooden heel. There were three basic types of heels: a solid wedge, a slightly curved wedge, and an extremely high arched heel sometimes referred to as the "southern split heel" or "double heel." While most heels were covered with plain fabric, some featured elaborate embroidery or couching. The under sole was lined with fine colored silk in the case of votive shoes and the tiny replicas used in religious rituals. Wearable shoes, however, were fitted with tiny leather tabs attached to the toe point, mid heel, and back heel with tiny metal or bamboo nails.

The colors of Cantonese shoes included many bright as well as pastel hues. For celebratory, votive, and party shoes, a favorite color combination was a red body with green or light blue heels. Another common color was mauve, which created a perfect backdrop for brightly colored designs of lotus flowers and chickens in colors of yellow, orange, green, red, and pink. Other colors used for the uppers included mint green, purple, emerald green, royal blue, turquoise blue, orange, salmon, and cream.

The popularity of the classic Cantonese shoe began to wane during the early years of the twentieth century when many younger women adopted simpler styles similar to those worn in central China. However, many of the tiny classic Cantonese shoes, as small as three to four inches in length, continued to be worn by older women in the villages for nearly thirty years longer before they finally disappeared before World War II.

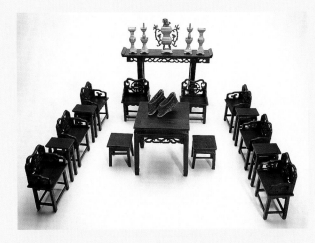

FIGURE 76

Cantonese votive shoes and altar furniture used in the ceremony of the Seven Heavenly Maidens, Zhongshan area, Guangdong province, 1910. The Seven Heavenly Maidens festival celebrated sisterhood and women's needlework. The "double seven" day—the seventh day of the seventh month—was the annual reunion of the Weaving Maid (the star Vega) and her husband the Cowherd (the star Altair). Two miniature seats were reserved for them in front of the altar table. Young women pledged friendship to each other as "seven sisters," and together they displayed needles and thread, toiletry items, and prized embroidery including seven pairs of votive shoes on the altar. Brought by a Cantonese immigrant woman, Mrs. Yuen Yun Kong, to Hawaii in the 1920s and used in ceremonies until the 1950s. Length of votive shoes: 7 cm (2¼ in.). Collection of Douglas D. L. Chong.

Miniature furniture in carved wood, miniature candlesticks and vases in pewter. Collection of Hawaii Plantation Village, Waipahu Cultural Garden Park.

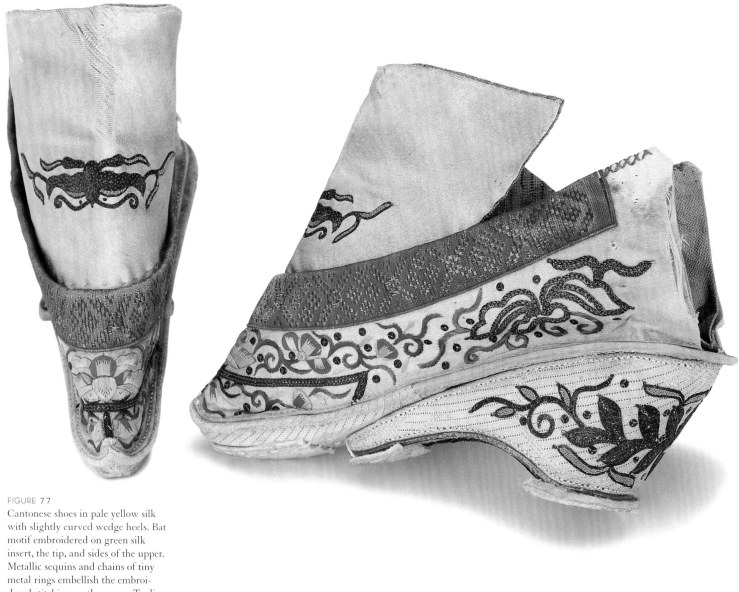

FIGURE 77
Cantonese shoes in pale yellow silk
with slightly curved wedge heels. Bat
motif embroidered on green silk
insert, the tip, and sides of the upper.
Metallic sequins and chains of tiny
metal rings embellish the embroidered stitching on the upper. Topline
edged with damask-darned stitching
in red and golden thread. Length:
12.8 cm (5 in.), late 19th century.
BSM P81.0075.AB.

arched, and made of cotton or hemp. The structure of Huizhou shoes is akin to a typical southern shoe from Jiangsu and Zhejiang, neighboring regions to the southeast, but the surface decoration shows distinct local flavor.

Datong City, in the northwestern Shanxi province, is another place where we find a large repertoire of local styles. Although there is a range of materials and design employed in Datong shoes, most characteristic is the downward sloping topline, often accented by a thick eye-catching trim that extends from heel to toe. The sharp arch of the decorated topline harmonizes with the arched wooden sole, directing the viewer's eyes to the pointy tip of the toe area. Datong shoes are marked by elaborate and creative designs of the upper; the women were so proud of their artistic creations that they took to exhibiting their shoes in temple fairs. These public displays sealed the fame of the city as a mecca of footbinding in the nineteenth and twentieth centuries.

Huizhou and Datong maintained their distinct styles, which became hallmarks of the regions' identities in the surrounding areas. Other cities developed a range of styles that crossbred with those from the neighboring areas, gradually creating regional styles that transcend any one locale. An example of this process is a trio of cities in the heartland of sericulture in China—Ningbo, Shaoxing, and Suzhou—where many of the Jiang-Zhe (*Jiang*su and *Zhe*jiang provinces) styles originated. Among the myriad lotus shoes from this fertile Yangzi delta area are two distinct archetypes—the elongated "ladder rung" (*wangzi xie*) and the low-heel pump, with or without the attached arclike insert above the toe area. Both types feature flexible two-piece cloth-covered soles, sometimes with kidney-shaped heels. Refined embroidery and elegant balance of colors on the satin uppers are hallmarks of these Jiang-Zhe shoes. Also noteworthy is the pastel-colored satin used for the "ladder rung" shoes, lending an air of delicacy to these soft-sided slippers.

In the southernmost tip of the empire, Guangdong province developed a regional style marked by vivid colors, wedged wooden heels, woven damask-darned topline with geometric patterns, and generous use of gold foil and thread. Douglas D. L. Chong, a descendant of Cantonese immigrants to Hawaii, has studied the characteristics of Cantonese lotus shoes in the context of footbinding rituals in southern China, Hawaii, and America (see "The Cantonese Lotus Shoes Defined").

THE SPEAKING SHOE

It is not an exaggeration to conclude that a tiny lotus shoe opens the door to a vast and meaningful world. As a product of a woman's hands, lotus shoes are testimonials of their maker's artistic talent and skills. In turn, the shape and construction of the shoes provide clues to how they affected the wearer's body. This is hardly surprising, in light of the fact that the lotus shoes were considered the most private and intimate aspect of a woman. Perhaps more remarkable is the extent to which the shoes for bound feet comprised an integral part of local artistic traditions and regional cultures.

How did private objects from the boudoir become vested with such public meanings? More research is needed to illuminate the stylistic influence of one local shoe-making tradition on another before this question can be answered in full. But this much is clear: women with bound feet were not cloistered creatures with wasted lives. In working on—and with—their bodies, they invested the shoe with personal and communal meanings that continue to speak to us long after the hands and feet have been laid to rest.

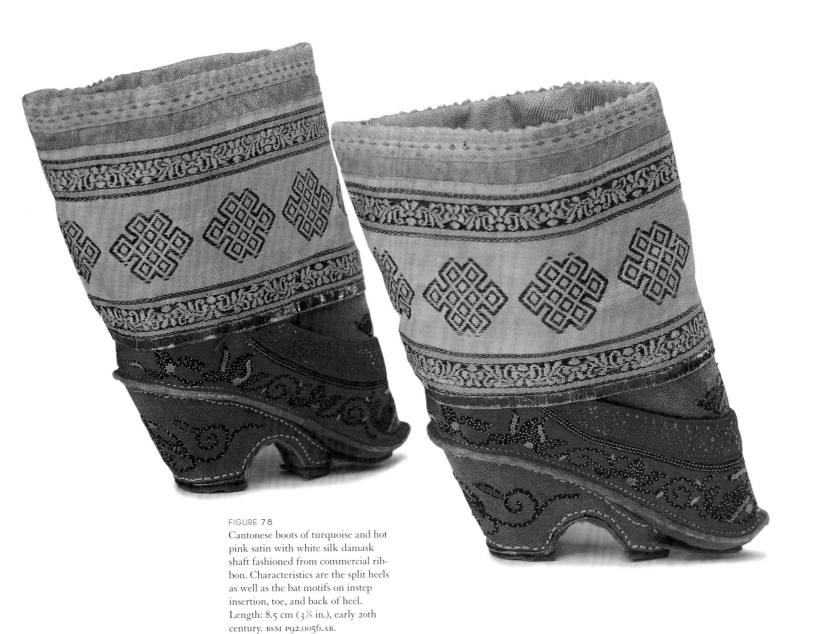

FIGURE 7 8
Cantonese boots of turquoise and hot
pink satin with white silk damask
shaft fashioned from commercial ribbon. Characteristics are the split heels
as well as the bat motifs on instep
insertion, toe, and back of heel.
Length: 8.5 cm (3⅜ in.), early 20th
century. BSM P92.0056.AB.

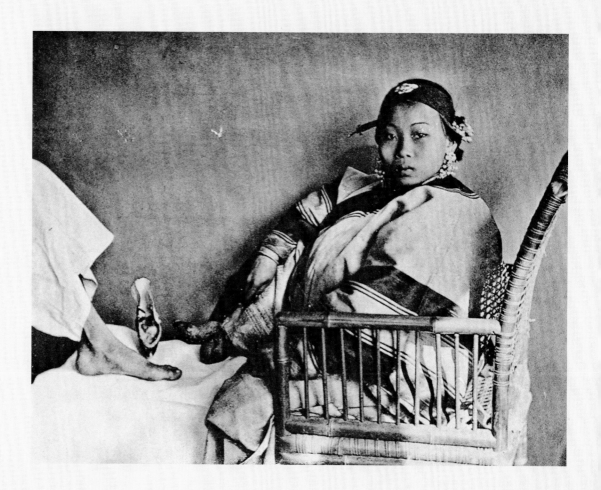

FIGURE 79
The Bound Foot of a Chinese Lady,
ca. 1870. From Thomson, *Illustra-*
tions of China and Its People.

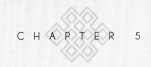

CHAPTER 5

A New World

I<small>N</small> 1865 <small>A</small> S<small>COTTISH</small> <small>TRAVELER</small>, John Thomson, opened a photographic studio in Singapore during his second trip to the East. About three years later he arrived in Hong Kong with his bulky equipment and set off to explore China with an army of porters carrying an entire darkroom fashioned from a tent. For four years he took photographs using the wet collodion process on the southern coast, along the Yangzi river, and up north all the way to Peking.

N<small>EW</small> E<small>YES</small>

Thomson was not the first photographer to work in China, nor was he the first to capture a glimpse of the bare bound foot. But with the publication of his *Illustrations of China and Its People* in 1873/74, a four-volume work with two hundred photographs of China in collotype prints, readers in Europe and Asia alike acquired new eyes with which to view China. The Chinese kingdom and its women would never look the same again.

A pioneer in using photography as social documentation, Thomson displayed a detached and realistic tone in his work, and this example is no exception. With economy he staged the scene to convey a basic fact about footbinding: the contrast in size between the foot of the female and that of a male tells the story about gender distinction. For virtually all of his readers at the time, the image was a revelation; precious few men—European or Chinese—had been privileged to set eyes on the naked skin of a woman with bound feet. The novelty of the image is significant. The focal point of footbinding was no longer the "packaging" of the foot and the display of women's handiwork—the layers of perfumed and embroidered binders, lotus shoes, leggings, sashes, and pants. The fixation had shifted to the naked flesh and bones. The photographic lens not only discovered footbinding, but had in this very discovery invented a brave new world of novel images and meanings. The lens was a new pair of eyes that engendered a new way of seeing.

The stripping of the binders appears to us a prerequisite for scientific study and documentation; eager are we to get at the inner truth of the matter. To the nameless woman in Amoy (Xiamen) who modeled for Thomson, however, it signaled unabashed humiliation. Probably too poor to resist a bribe, she lost control over the way her body and image were to be presented to the world. In the decades that followed, new authorities such as missionary doctors and anthropologists persistently peeled away the binding cloth to study and document the custom. Without detracting from the value of these scientific projects, which produced the bulk of contemporary knowledge about footbinding, we should recognize an inevitable side effect: the exposure and scrutiny of the naked feet spelled the end of footbinding as we know it, a practice that thrived on the mystique of concealment and the spectacle of shoes.

OLD CHINA

I do not intend to suggest that the investigations of the photographer or ethnographer caused the downfall of a millennial-old custom. Global shifts in

the nineteenth century altered the economic position of China in such fundamental ways that the premise of Chinese culture came to be questioned. Footbinding became a stand-in for everything that was wrong about "tradition,"
especially its family structure and gender politics. This national identification,
by its sheer public nature, transformed the meanings of a practice that had
thrived on women's private knowledge, labor, rituals, and artistry.

These same decades when footbinding was subjected to global scrutiny—
the 1860s to 1910s—saw an increasingly vocal effort on the part of foreign
missionaries and Chinese reformers to end footbinding. Their efforts, under
the rubric of the anti-footbinding or natural foot movements, have received
much scholarly attention. To my mind, it was not these organized campaigns
in themselves but the frequent exposure of the bound feet in town halls and
school assemblies that was most instrumental in altering the fate of footbinding. Recent scholars who have analyzed the local anti-footbinding societies
reveal that most of these organized elite efforts were woefully ineffective in
changing female behavior and values. The rhetoric of national salvation they
used was appealing to a sector of reform-minded men and women. But
nationalism was their agenda; mothers with bound feet had other priorities
and concerns.

Although footbinding ended rapidly in the coastal cities, elsewhere in
China and among certain regional population sectors the practice continued
well into the 1930s and 1940s. In such remote areas as Yunnan, footbinding
did not end until the late 1950s under a coercive communist campaign. In all
provinces that launched state-run anti-footbinding campaigns during the first
half of the twentieth century, women with bound feet threw foot inspectors
from their bedrooms or paid a fine to rid themselves of the intruders; girls
ran off to hide in the mountains. Why did they refuse to be "liberated"? It is
too simplistic to dismiss them as victims of tradition hindering the progress of
modernity. In many cases the women were resisting the encroachment of the

state into their private lives, or outsiders dictating what they should do with their own bodies. Why would they submit to a campaign that derided them as wasted and wasteful, crippled and lazy? The woman with bound feet—many people championed her salvation, but who would walk a mile in her shoes?

New Shoes

Once we shift focus from male to female agendas, and from exposed flesh back to the shoes, we may see that the transitional period from the 1890s to 1920s was in fact an extremely inventive one in the styles and workmanship of lotus shoes. The infusion of new materials and techniques, as well as the invention of new styles, was nothing short of revolutionary. To the extent that footbinding had always been about fashion, not much had changed. But the new-style lotus shoes are unmistakably products of a new commercialized economy and a modern fashion culture.

Some lotus shoes were "modernized," in step with new tastes. Chinese fashion plates from the 1910s began to depict stylish young women dressed in Western-style leather mid-heel pumps. It was not so much the style but the material that signaled the novelty: lotus shoes from many regions had been outfitted with elegant high heels, but leather is a new material seldom found on lotus shoes made before the twentieth century. Although lotus shoes made entirely of leather were rare, leather lifts and reinforcements became common on twentieth-century lotus shoes that otherwise retained their traditional look. The ease with which new materials were incorporated into existing designs bespeaks a vitality in the shoe-making industry, which produced many hybrid styles, old and new, as well as in between.

The same hybridity is evident in another group of modern lotus shoes called "pointy tip" (*jianzui xie*). Although their satin uppers with embroidered floral motifs rivaled traditional lotus shoes in refinement, these shoes were influenced by the Western principle of symmetrical footwear. Popular in the fashionable treaty ports in the late 1920s and 1930s, pointy tips were the first lotus shoes to feature distinct left and right pairings. Other new elements, such as button closures and "Mary Jane" cross straps, also lent a "Western chic" appearance. The one-piece upper construction departs from traditional lotus shoes, which are usually wrought of two-piece uppers.

Women with bound feet could make a fashion statement by wearing pointy tips without sacrificing comfort. Although the tip was extremely slender, the shallow vamp allowed the bulk of the wearer's foot to sit outside the shoe. The wide heel area and flat soles also enhanced movement. Women whose feet were narrow, with four folded digits but without a drastically bent arch, would find these shoes a welcome change from high heels. They included older women who let out their feet but kept the binders on and young women who bound lightly.

FIGURE 80
Shoes for bound feet in leather from the early to mid-twentieth century.

From left to right:
Leather shoe with elastic gusset on side. Stacked leather heel and leather sole. Yellow machine stitching at seams. Length: 14.5 cm (5¾ in.). BSM P84.0040.

Black patent leather shoe with instep strap and leather sole. Length: 16 cm (6¼ in.). BSM S79.0069.

Black leather shoe with instep strap and stacked leather heels. Length: 16.6 cm (6½ in.). Collection of Dr. Chi-sheng Ko.

Black leather Oxford with cotton laces. Length: 19 cm (7½ in.). BSM P01.30.

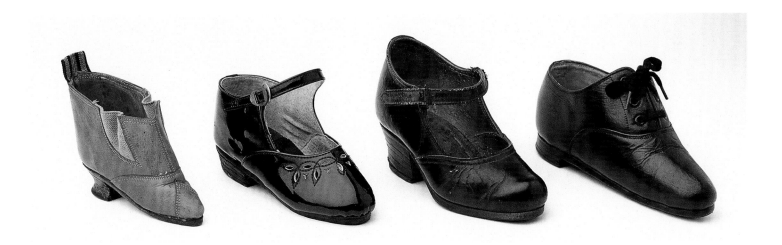

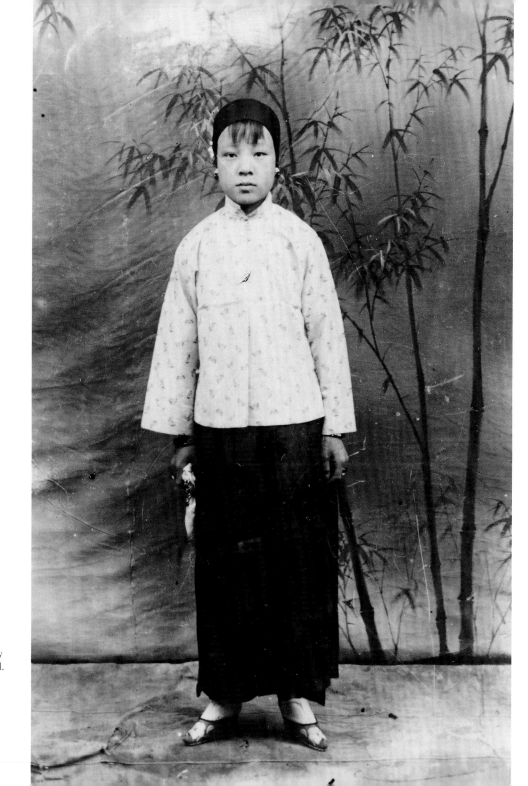

Teenage girl in Western-influenced
lotus shoes. She stands in a distinctly
untraditional pose, with feet splayed.
1910s–1920s. Courtesy of Dr.
Chi-sheng Ko.

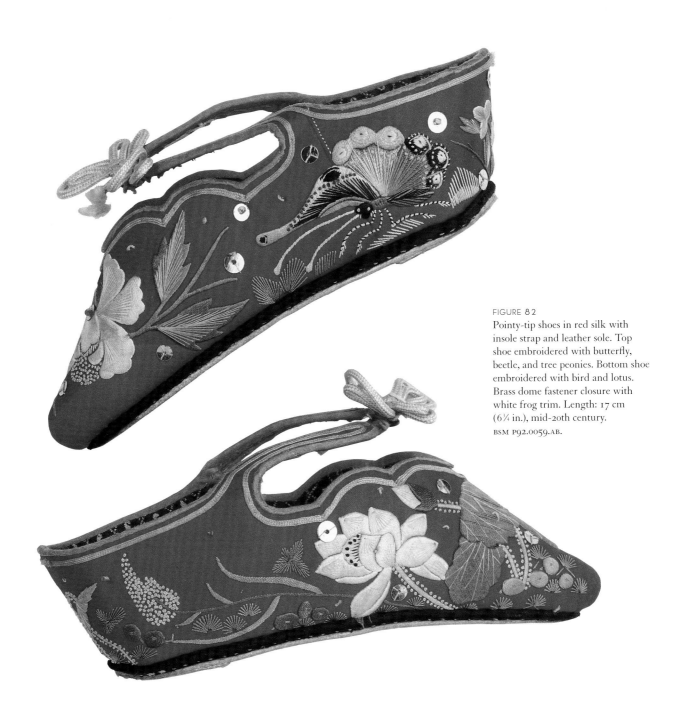

FIGURE 82
Pointy-tip shoes in red silk with insole strap and leather sole. Top shoe embroidered with butterfly, beetle, and tree peonies. Bottom shoe embroidered with bird and lotus. Brass dome fastener closure with white frog trim. Length: 17 cm (6¼ in.), mid-20th century.
BSM P92.0059.AB.

Other hybrid elements are more subtle, but they indicate fundamental changes in shoe production in the urban half of the country. The use of leather and machine stitching signaled the complete removal of shoe-making from domestic production. In 1920s Shanghai, professional shoe-makers visited fashionable ladies in their homes with sample fabrics and embroidery designs to take orders and measurements. The shoes were then manufactured in the shop and delivered to the clients. One such shoe-maker, whose moniker was "The Vegetarian," became famous for improvising designs from his client's verbal descriptions. He was among the first to establish a storefront with a workshop in the back.[1] In the less commercialized areas and the hinterland, women continued to make shoes in the time-tested ways. But they, too, were in tune with the times. Fabrics woven in factories and dyed bright magenta, turquoise, or pink with imported chemicals found their way to the countryside, creating a new aesthetic of color; cheap cotton or polyester fabrics with machine-stamped patterns were increasingly used as lining for the upper and insole.

Living through tumultuous times in the early decades of the twentieth century, women with bound feet quietly made adjustments. "Letting feet out" was in fact a relative term; for most women it meant less vigilance and a looser binding. In due time the feet would expand and straighten somewhat, but for many women the best way to retain their stride was to keep the binders on. Without fanfare, the majority of women with bound feet kept on working with their hands and feet—in the dry fields, in the silk workshops, at home on the *kang* platform bed. Modern women with big feet puttered around the city, wasting time in dancing halls and cinemas. Not them. They must work and would work until the day they died; that was the woman's lot and nothing had changed as far as they were concerned.

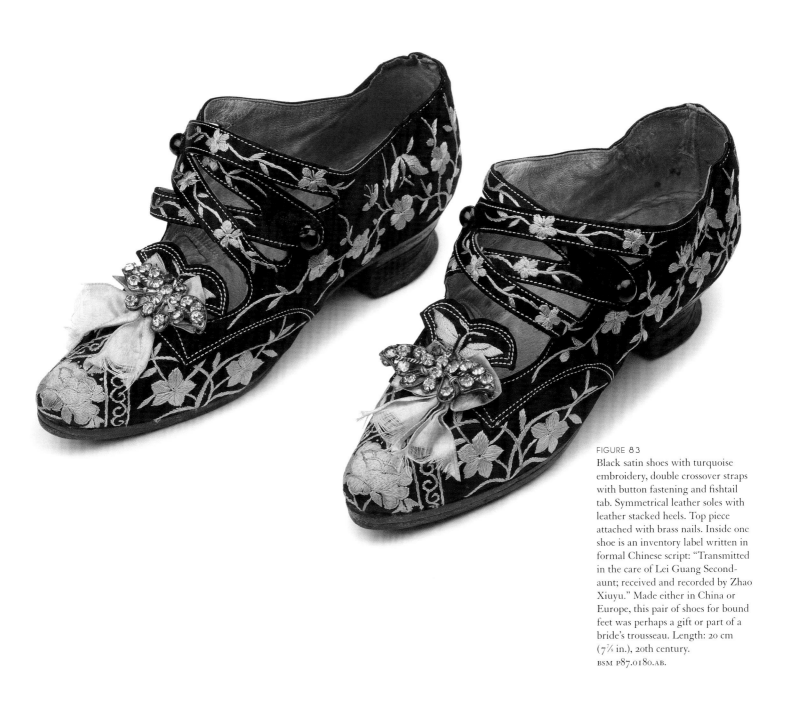

FIGURE 83

Black satin shoes with turquoise embroidery, double crossover straps with button fastening and fishtail tab. Symmetrical leather soles with leather stacked heels. Top piece attached with brass nails. Inside one shoe is an inventory label written in formal Chinese script: "Transmitted in the care of Lei Guang Second-aunt; received and recorded by Zhao Xiuyu." Made either in China or Europe, this pair of shoes for bound feet was perhaps a gift or part of a bride's trousseau. Length: 20 cm (7⅞ in.), 20th century.
BSM P87.0180.AB.

NEW LANDS

The resilience of women with bound feet is striking in light of what they had to overcome. In hindsight, it is clear to us that the decline of footbinding was inevitable given the global forces aligned against it. This makes it all the more remarkable that on the eve of its decline, footbinding underwent yet another significant shift as it became an overseas Chinese practice. In the second half of the nineteenth century, women who migrated to Southeast Asia and the New World brought with them not only their lotus shoes but also the repertoire of rituals, values, and skills associated with binding. Ironically, it was not until then, in the age of nascent nationalism, and in places thousands of miles away from China, that footbinding became firmly identified with Chinese culture as a whole. No longer embedded in local regional cultures or ethnic politics (Han versus Manchu), footbinding, for better or worse, became the marker of Chinese femininity in the same way that the queue became the marker of Chinese masculinity.

The fate of footbinding outside China varied greatly according to the number of women immigrants, their economic status, prevailing

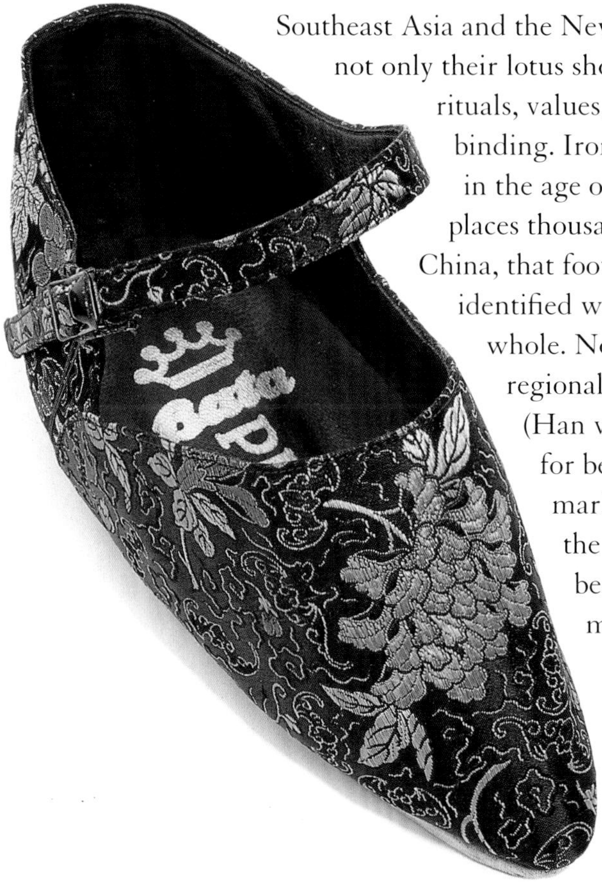

FIGURE 84
Lotus shoe for the market in Southeast Asia. Brocade shoe with instep strap with stitched felt sole. "Bata Princess" perforation in sock. This line of footwear was sold to women with feet that had been bound and then let out as late as the 1950s in Singapore. An estimated fifty to one hundred pairs of each style were made. Length: 17 cm (6¾ in.).
BSM S79.0068.

customs in their native place, and the attitudes of those in the host countries. There are reports that merchant wives in the Philippines signaled their elite status with bound feet. Chinese settlers in Singapore and Malacca, then parts of the British colony of Malaya, also continued the practice. Bata Princess shoes, a fashionable line of commercial footwear, supplied the needs of these women, as did shoe makers with their own shops. Made of machine-woven brocade, these shoes bear little resemblance to the lotus shoes seen so far, but we can make out the shape of the bound foot from the pointed tip and the bulging arch. The last maker of lotus shoes in Malacca, Yeo Sing Guat, closed his doors only in the 1980s. Yeo grew up in a cobbler's family that supplied shoes to Chinese women with bound feet, but when his last client reached one hundred years of age, he turned his skills to the creation of "lotus shoe" souvenirs for tourists.

Women from southern China traveled to lands beyond Southeast Asia with hopes of improving the lives of their families. During the late nineteenth century, wives with bound feet from Zhongshan county of Guangdong settled in the Kingdom of Hawaii. Some remained faithful to the practice and bound the feet of their Hawaii-born daughters despite a ban by the king. Douglas D. L. Chong, a fifth-generation Chinese American son, recalls the small size of his grandmother's feet and the classic Guangdong-style shoes she made. In the family homestead in Kaluanui, Punaluu, on the island of Oahu, where the family operated a rice plantation, his great-grandmother, Mrs. Ching Kan You, personally bound her four older daughters' feet. The two youngest were spared because their brother intervened. All the women worked in the fields, pounding rice, chopping wood, growing vegetables, and raising pigs, chickens, and ducks. In another nearby rice-farming community, settlers from a neighboring village in Zhongshan engaged the services of a professional footbinder.[2]

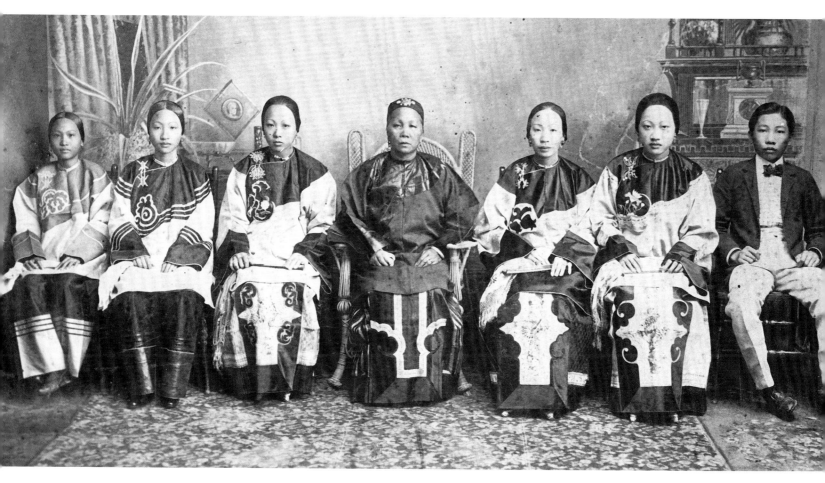

FIGURE 85

Mrs. Ching Kan You and her children. Left to right: Mrs. Tom You, Mrs. Luke See Chin, Mrs. Chun Mun Chu, Mrs. Ching Kan You, Mrs. Tom Chung, Mrs. Yuen Sock (Douglas Chong's grandmother), and Mr. Ching Hung Yau, the only son. He later attended the University of Southern California and the Michigan College of Mining Engineering. One daughter is not present. The four older daughters had their feet bound in childhood. Honolulu, Hawaii, 1902. Courtesy of Douglas D. L. Chong.

OLD SHOES, NEW MEANINGS

The age of decline witnessed another new development in the history of footbinding—the birth of private collections and antique markets of lotus shoes. Before the nineteenth century, although handmade shoes were treasured by the women who made them, and by their relatives and friends, there is no indication that shoes were collector's items with a history and value transcending the lives of the women. The curiosity of foreign visitors, many of them missionaries who arrived in the interior of the empire in increasing numbers after 1860, coupled with entrepreneurial Chinese intent upon preserving traces of an antiquated practice for posterity, created an economy of supply and demand in lotus shoes. This became the basis of the majority of the collections in museums and private hands today.

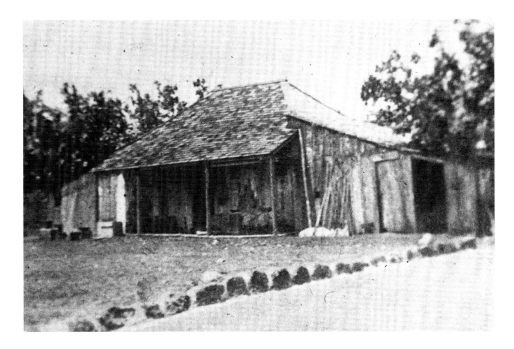

FIGURE 86
The Ching family homestead in Kaluanui, Punaluu, Oahu, Hawaii, where the family lived from 1883 to 1911. In this dirt-floor farmhouse, Mrs. Ching Kan You bound her daughters' feet. Courtesy of Douglas D. L. Chong.

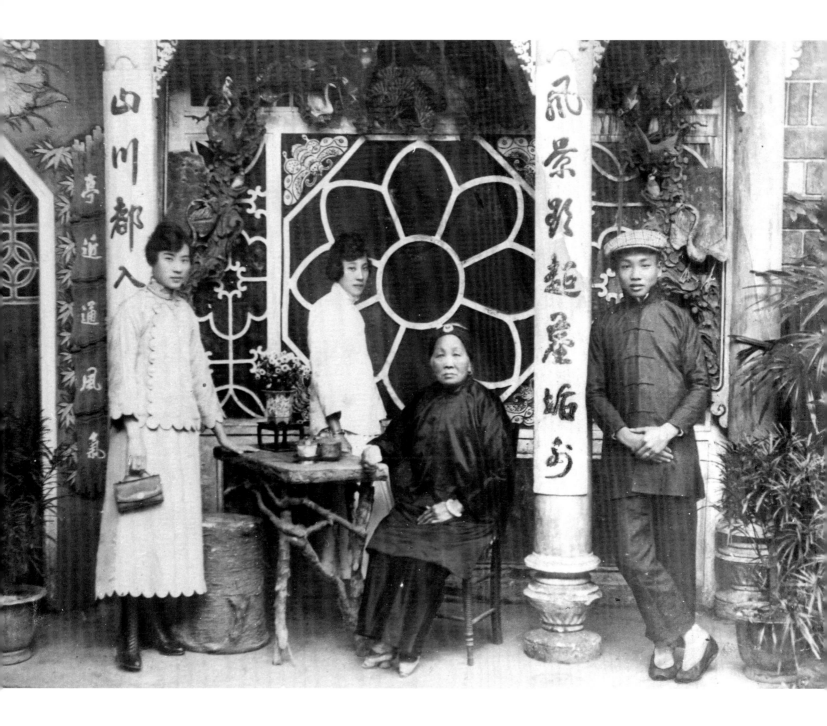

The way in which these collections were assembled affected our knowledge about shoes for bound feet. From the prehistoric shell mounds to Imelda Marcos's purchases, collecting is a human activity as old as it is diverse in motivations. But the museum with its professional curatorial staff and public educational mission is a distinctly modern institution. Any museum collection, be it amassed from personal travels, purchases from dealers, or private donation, is built with a particular vision and mission. It is purposeful and selective. Museum collections do not simply reflect what is "out there" in

FIGURE 87, OPPOSITE
Mrs. Ching Kan You, who migrated to Hawaii in 1880, is shown here in retirement in her native village of Xicun (Sai Chien), Nanlang (Nam Long), in southern China. To her left is her grandson. In contrast to her two granddaughters visiting from Hawaii in modern attire, her feet are still bound, and she wears the classic Cantonese shoes with sturdy guava-wood heels made by her husband twenty years earlier in Hawaii. Zhongshan county, Pearl River delta, 1919. Courtesy of Douglas D. L. Chong.

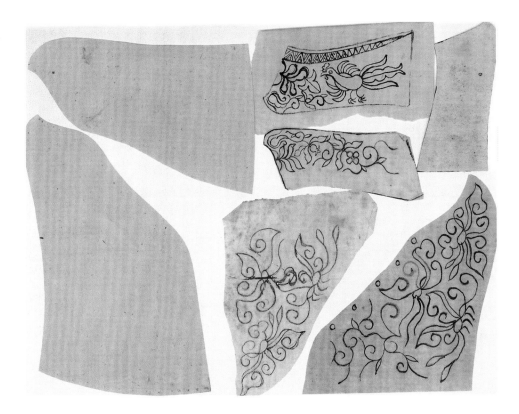

FIGURE 88
Cantonese-style shoe patterns, in sizes from tightly bound to let-out feet. Designed and used by the Ching family in Honolulu, Hawaii, 1889–1911. Courtesy of Douglas D. L. Chong.

FIGURE 89
Cantonese shoe components, green
and pink silk with gold couching
and satin-stitched embroidery. The
patterns were drawn on a piece of
American Cherokee writing tablet
paper, cut, and covered with silk.
The design on paper was then traced
onto the silk and embroidered. Made
by the Ching family in Honolulu,
Hawaii, 1898. Courtesy of Douglas
D. L. Chong.

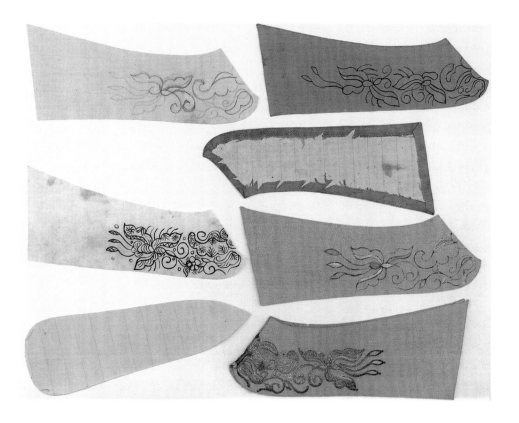

China; they generate new knowledge by assigning values to certain artifacts
over others and by labeling and classifying holdings in a standard scheme.

Due to the private nature of the subject matter, exhibitions of footbinding-
related artifacts are by definition exposés and thus controversial if not incendi-
ary. In the 1904 St. Louis Exposition, the Qing imperial government displayed
a number of arched shoes along with figurines of footbound women in its
pavilion to showcase the sophistication of traditional handicraft, oblivious to
the fact that prevailing world opinion did not find such "traditional craft"

admirable. Chinese students in the United States were incensed, adding impetus to the anti-Qing revolutionary forces at home, which toppled the dynasty and established a republic in 1912.[3] The identification of footbinding with national shame was thus sealed in many minds. As recently as 1992, a small exhibition of lotus shoes in a gallery in Taipei, Taiwan, incurred the wrath of some observers, who accused the organizers of sensationalizing women's pain.

As a historian who has studied footbinding and women's cultures for years, I do not claim to be neutral. I feel strongly that we should understand footbinding not as a senseless act of destruction but as a meaningful practice in the eyes of the women themselves. This stance, adopted throughout this book, has led me to focus on the lotus shoes themselves instead of the crushed bones. As carriers and expressions of family values, women's handiwork, good wishes, and regional cultures, lotus shoes of all sizes, shapes, and colors are not only beautiful but also deeply meaningful.

Only upon entering the women's material world do we realize that there was not one footbinding but many, as each woman made decisions about when and how to bind that best suited her aspirations and local circumstances. As much as we should strive to see the world from the women's eyes, in the end, however, we must admit that we live in a vastly different time and place than theirs. At this point, we may begin the journey anew by looking at footbinding with our own—albeit transformed—eyes. The lotus shoes comprise an open book that invites revisiting and reinterpretation, rewarding us with pleasure and renewed knowledge about ourselves in the process.

NOTES

Epigraph

"The Story of the Doe" (Lunü furen yuan), in *Zabaojang jing* (The Sutra on the Storehouse of Sundry Valuables). T. no. 203. In *Taishō shinshū daizōkyō* (The Tripitaka in Chinese), ed. Takakusu Junjirō and Watanabe Kaigyoku (Tokyo: Taishō Issaikyō kankōkai, 1924–34), 4:452–53.

Introduction

1   Ruth Rosen, "Draw the Line at the Knife," *Los Angeles Times*, 17 November 1991; Elizabeth Gleick, "Diary of a Dependent Spouse," *New York Times Magazine*, 9 August 1998.

2   Two classic feminist criticisms of footbinding are Andrea Dworkin, *Woman Hating* (New York: Plume, 1974); and Mary Daly, *Gyn/Ecology: The Metaethics of Radical Feminism* (Boston: Beacon Press, 1978).

3   *Body Play and Modern Primitives Quarterly* 5, no. 1 (1998). For a scholarly study of the subject, see the chapter "Shoes" in Valerie Steele, *Fetish: Fashion, Sex, and Power* (New Haven: Yale University Press, 1996).

4   For a pioneering attempt to study shoes for bound feet as part of material culture, see Valery M. Garrett, *Chinese Clothing: An Illustrated Guide* (Hong Kong: Oxford University Press, 1994). See also the discussion of women's and children's footwear in her *A Collector's Guide to Chinese Dress Accessories* (Singapore: Times Editions, 1997), pp. 135–55. Three private collectors of lotus shoes have published books or articles on their own collections. See bibliography for publications by Chisheng Ko, Glenn Roberts and Valerie Steele, and Beverley Jackson.

5   A recent study is Fan Hong, *Footbinding, Feminism, and Freedom: The Liberation of Women's Bodies in Modern China* (London: Frank Cass, 1997). Although useful as a study of the introduction of sports in China, this book sheds little light on footbinding, for the author has accepted uncritically the values of the anti-footbinding activists she studied. Chinese novelist Feng Jicai offers a vivid portrayal of the psychological conflict suffered by the older generation of women when footbinding ceased to be fashionable in his *Three Inch Golden Lotus* (Honolulu: University of Hawaii Press, 1994). In stark contrast to Fan Hong, another Chinese scholar, Wang Ping, who tried to bind her own feet during the Cultural Revolution, champions female desires in her *Aching for Beauty: Footbinding in China* (Minneapolis: University of Minnesota Press, 2000).

6   See, for example, William A. Rossi, *The Sex Life of the Foot and Shoe* (New York: Ballantine Books, 1978).

Chapter 1

1 The strip of cloth binding her feet is 9 cm (3½ in.) wide and 210 cm (82⅝ in.) long. The excavation report is *Fuzhou Nan-Song Huang Sheng mu* (The Southern Song dynasty tomb of Huang Sheng in Fuzhou) (Beijing: Wenwu chubanshe, 1982). For a study of the textile items unearthed, including the shoes and socks, see Dieter Kuhn, *Die Song-Dynastie: Eine neue Gesellschaft im Spiegel ihrer Kultur* (Weinheim: Acta Humaniora, VCH, 1987), pp. 331–75. I am grateful to Professor Kuhn and Dr. Ina Asim for making this text available to me.

2 Quzhoushi wenguan hui, "Zhejiang Quzhoushi Nan-Song mu chutu qiwu" (Artifacts unearthed from the Southern Song tomb in Quzhou city, Zhejiang province), *Kaogu* 11 (1983): 1004–11, 1018. See the discussion in English in Patricia Ebrey, *The Inner Quarters: Marriage and the Lives of Chinese Women in the Sung Period* (Berkeley and Los Angeles: University of California Press, 1993), pp. 37–43.

3 Li Keyou et al., "Jiangxi De'an Nan-Song Zhoushi mu qingli jianbao" (A brief report of the clearing of the tomb of Madame Zhou in De'an city, Jiangxi province), *Wenwu* 9 (1990): 1–13. See discussion of the tomb in Dieter Kuhn, *A Place for the Dead: An Archaeological Documentary on Graves and Tombs of the Song Dynasty (960–1279)* (Heidelberg: Edition Forum, 1996), pp. 143–45. Another pair of shoes

from a Southern Song dynasty tomb in Lanxi, Zhejiang, is comparable in length (17 cm; 6¾ in.) and width (5.8 cm; 2¼ in.) to Madame Zhou's. Gao Hongxing, *Chanzu shi* (A history of footbinding) (Shanghai: Shanghai wenyi chubanshe, 1995), p. 19.

4 Cao Zijian, "Rhapsody on the Luo River Goddess," in Xiao Tong, *Wen xuan, or Selections of Refined Literature*, translated by David R. Knechtges (Princeton: Princeton University Press, 1996), 3:355–65. The Chinese river nymph is often depicted as a dragon frolicking in clouds and rain. The meeting of the goddess and her shaman-king is often a sexual encounter, and "clouds and rain" became a euphemism for sexual intercourse. See Edward Schafer, *The Divine Woman: Dragon Ladies and Rain Maidens* (San Francisco: North Point Press, 1980).

5 *Quan Tang shi* (Complete Tang poetry) (Shanghai: Shanghai guji, 1995), p. 1719.

6 This story first appeared in an official history compiled during the Tang dynasty, *History of the Southern Dynasties*. But it became part of the footbinding lore after Song scholar Zhang Bangji made the connection in his *Mozhuang manlu* (Random notes from the Ink Estate), 8.5a-b, in *Siku quanshu*, Zi bu 10, Zajia lei 3. *Mozhuang manlu* was completed around 1174.

7 Ouyang Yuqian, ed., *Tangdai wudao* (Dance cultures of the Tang dynasty) (Taipei: Lanting, 1985), pp. 11, 115–19. The Tazhi dance remained popular into the succeeding Song dynasty, but it was turned into a much less provocative ensemble of scores of dancers, interspersed with singing and recitations. See Yuan He, *Zhongguo wudao yixiang lun* (A study of the concepts and aesthetics of Chinese dance) (Beijing: Wenhua yishu, 1994), pp. 158–61.

8 Ouyang, *Tangdai wudao*, pp. 100–101.

9 Yin Yazhao, *Zhongguo gudian yu minwu yanjiu* (A study of classical and folk dance in China) (Taipei: Guanya, 1991), p. 169. For the Rainbow Skirt and Feathered Cape dance in general, see pp. 161–78.

10 Gao Hongxing, *Chanzu shi*, p. 7.

11 It is possible that the Yaoniang story first appeared earlier. The complete story cited here is from scholar Tao Zongyi's (1320–1400) *Chuogeng lu* (Resting the plough), 10.16a–b, in *Siku quanshu*, Zi bu 12, Xiaoshuojia lei 1. Tao attributed the story to another source, *Daoshan xinwen*, which is no longer extant. In the thirteenth century, scholar Zhou Mi (1232–1308) mentioned a palace dancer in the Later Tang court who bound her feet into a new moon shape, but he did not give the details in Tao's account. In *Huoran zhai yadan*, Zhou attributed the story to an anonymous source; see Ebrey, *Inner Quarters*, p. 38.

12   Xu Zhi, *Jiexiao ji* (Deeds of integrity and filial piety), 14.7a, in *Siku quanshu*, Ji bu 3, Bieji lei 2.

CHAPTER 2

1   On the average, a seven-*sui* Chinese girl would be six years old by Western count, but this is only an approximate rule of thumb. If a girl was born late in the lunar year and had her feet bound early in a lunar year, she would be almost two years younger by Western reckoning than her "age at binding" measured in *sui*. For age reckoning and the female life course, see Susan Mann, *Precious Records: Women in China's Long Eighteenth Century* (Stanford: Stanford University Press, 1997), pp. 45–75.

2   Hu Pu'an, *Zhonghua quanguo fengsuzhi* (Local customs in China) (Hebei: Hebei Renmin, 1986), 2:164. The same day is also known to farmers as the birthday of the rice plant. For the Tiny-Footed Maiden, see also Howard S. Levy, *Chinese Footbinding: The History of a Curious Erotic Custom* (Taipei: Southern Materials Center, 1984), p. 57.

3   In Buddhism, a bodhisattva is one who follows the way of the Buddha and who seeks enlightenment by way of wisdom and compassion. Guanyin (meaning "Observer of the sounds of the world") is equally popular as Kannon in Japan. See Chün-fang Yü, *Kuan-yin: The Chinese Transformation of Avalokiteśvara* (New York: Columbia University Press, 2001).

4   For these stories see Chün-fang Yü, "Guanyin: The Chinese Transformation of Avalokiteśvara," in *Latter Days of the Law: Images of Chinese Buddhism, 850–1850*, ed. Marsha Weidner (Honolulu: University of Hawaii, 1994), pp. 150–81.

5   For the White-Robed Guanyin and the related cult of the Buddha's mother, see Yü, "Guanyin."

6   *Mingyuan shigui cao* (Poetic retrospective of famous ladies) (n.p., n.d.), no page. Handwritten manuscript in the Tōyō Bunko, Tokyo, Japan.

CHAPTER 3

1   For silk goddesses and silk production, see Dieter Kuhn, *Textile Technology: Spinning and Reeling*, vol. 5, pt. 9 of *Science and Civilisation in China*, ed. Joseph Needham (Cambridge: Cambridge University Press, 1988).

2   For a comparison of textile production and consumption between China and Europe, see Kenneth Pomeranz, *The Great Divergence: China, Europe, and the Making of the Modern World Economy* (Princeton: Princeton University Press, 2000), pp. 327–38. Susan Mann has studied the relationship between the spread of cotton and footbinding, in *Precious Records*. Anthropologist Hill Gates, in turn, has argued that footbinding spread with "petty capitalist commercialization," and went into

decline as China encountered capitalist-industrialism. See her "Footbinding and Handspinning in Sichuan," in *Constructing China*, ed. Ernest P. Young (Ann Arbor: AAS Monographs, 1998), pp. 177–94. See also by Gates, "On a New Footing: Footbinding and the Coming of Modernity," *Research on Women in Modern Chinese History* 5 (August 1997): 115–36.

3   Ethnographers from the Hong Kong Heritage Museum have interviewed old makers of lotus shoes. Photographs of the shoe-making process reenacted according to the memory of an eighty-some-year-old Madam Tsui Mei-wah are in Naomi Yin-yin Szeto, *Of Hearts and Hands: Hong Kong's Traditional Trades and Crafts* (Hong Kong: The Urban Council, 1996), pp. 70–73. Madam Tsui, a native of Shandong, had her feet bound at age five and learned shoe-making from her grandmother.

4   For the story and poems of Shen Yixiu and her daughters, see my *Teachers of the Inner Chambers*, pp. 206–7.

5   Ding Pei, *Xiu pu* (The way of embroidery), *sheng*.17a.

CHAPTER 5

1   Gan Gu, ed., *Shanghai bainian ming-chang laodian* (Famous centuries-old factories and stores in Shanghai) (Shanghai: Shanghai wenhua chubanshe, 1987), p. 111. I thank Professor Luo Suwen for calling this to my attention.

2   Violet L. Lai, *He Was a Ram: Wong Aloiau of Hawaii* (Honolulu: Published for the Hawaii Chinese History Center and the Wong Aloiau Association by the University of Hawaii Press, 1985). Douglas Dai Lunn Chong, *Ancestral Reflections: Hawaii's Early Chinese of Waipahu, An Ethnic Community Experience, 1885–1935* (Waipahu, Hawaii: Waipahu Tsoong Nyee Society, 1998).

3   Also on display were opium implements, another symbol of national shame in the eyes of the nationalists. I am indebted to Susan R. Fernsebner for information on the St. Louis Expo. In her pioneer research on Chinese participation in world fairs, she has found that in the Centennial Exhibition of 1876 in Philadelphia, "one would find women's 'small footed' shoes listed with various other footwear items, both men and women's, alongside deerskin boots, silk hats, 'ear caps,' and oxhide moccasins. In 1904, however, they were no longer mere products but, framed within an anthropological discourse of progress and civilization, had been transformed into both curiosities and concrete representations of national disgrace." Chapter 1 of "Material Modernities: China's Participation in World's Fairs and Expositions" (Ph.D. diss., University of California at San Diego, 2002).

BIBLIOGRAPHY

Body Play and Modern Primitives Quarterly 5, no. 1 (1998).

Bray, Francesca. *Technology and Gender: Fabrics of Power in Late Imperial China*. Berkeley and Los Angeles: University of California Press, 1997.

Cao, Zijian. "Rhapsody on the Luo River Goddess." In Xiao Tong, *Wen xuan, or Selections of Refined Literature*, translated by David R. Knechtges, 3:355–65. Princeton: Princeton University Press, 1996.

China: The Land and Its People: Early Photographs by John Thomson. Hong Kong: John Warner Publications, 1977.

Chinese Costumes. Pts. 1 and 2. In *Five Thousand Years of Chinese Art Series*. Taipei: The Five Thousand Years of Chinese Art Editorial Committee, 1986.

Chong, Douglas Dai Lunn. *Ancestral Reflections: Hawaii's Early Chinese of Waipahu, An Ethnic Community Experience, 1885–1935*. Waipahu, Hawaii: Waipahu Tsoong Nyee Society, 1998.

Daly, Mary. *Gyn/Ecology: The Metaethics of Radical Feminism*. Boston: Beacon Press, 1978.

Dennis G. Crow Ltd. *Historic Photographs of Hong Kong, Canton, and Macao: Catalog for an Exhibition and Sale at the Museum Annex, One Exchange Square, Hong Kong, 23 June 1998–30 June 1998*. Hong Kong: Dennis G. Crow, 1998.

Ding, Pei. *Xiu pu* (The way of embroidery). N.p., 1821.

Duan, Chengshi. *Youyang zazu* (Miscellanies from Youyang). In *Siku quanshu*, Zi bu 12, Xiaoshuojia lei 3.

Dworkin, Andrea. *Woman Hating*. New York: Plume, 1974.

Ebrey, Patricia. *The Inner Quarters: Marriage and the Lives of Chinese Women in the Sung Period*. Berkeley and Los Angeles: University of California Press, 1993.

Fan, Hong. *Footbinding, Feminism, and Freedom: The Liberation of Women's Bodies in Modern China*. London: Frank Cass, 1997.

Feng, Jicai. *Three Inch Golden Lotus*. Honolulu: University of Hawaii Press, 1994.

Fernsebner, Susan R. "Material Modernities: China's Participation in World's Fairs and Expositions." Ph.D. diss., Department of History, University of California at San Diego, 2002.

Fuzhou Nan-Song Huang Sheng mu (The Southern Song dynasty tomb of Huang Sheng in Fuzhou). Beijing: Wenwu chubanshe, 1982.

Gan, Bao. *Soushen ji* (Compendium of the gods). In *Huitu Sanjiao yuanliu soushen daquan* (Complete illustrated compendium of the gods of the three religions), 432–33. Shanghai: Shanghai guji, 1990.

Gan, Gu, ed. *Shanghai bainian mingchang laodian* (Famous centuries-old factories and stores in Shanghai). Shanghai: Shanghai wenhua chubanshe, 1987.

Gao, Hongxing. *Chanzu shi* (A history of footbinding). Shanghai: Shanghai wenyi chubanshe, 1995.

Garrett, Valery M. *Chinese Clothing: An Illustrated Guide*. Hong Kong: Oxford University Press, 1994.

———. *A Collector's Guide to Chinese Dress Accessories*. Singapore: Times Editions, 1997.

Gates, Hill. "On a New Footing: Footbinding and the Coming of Modernity." *Research on Women in Modern Chinese History* 5 (August 1997): 115–36.

———. "Footbinding and Handspinning in Sichuan." In *Constructing China*, edited by Ernest P. Young, 177–94. Ann Arbor: AAS Monographs, 1998.

Gleick, Elizabeth. "Diary of a Dependent Spouse." *New York Times Magazine*, 9 August 1998.

Hu, Pu'an. *Zhonghua quanguo fengsuzhi* (Local customs in China). Vol. 2. Hebei: Hebei Renmin, 1986.

Jackson, Beverley. *Splendid Slippers: A Thousand Years of an Erotic Tradition*. Berkeley: Ten Speed Press, 1997.

Knapp, Ronald G. *China's Living Houses: Folk Beliefs, Symbols, and Household Ornamentation*. Honolulu: University of Hawaii Press, 1999.

Ko, Chi-sheng. *Sancun jinlian: Oumi, maili jinji* (The three-inch golden lotus: Mystery, enchantment, and taboo). Taipei: Zhanye qingbao zazi she, 1995.

———. *Shengui hongyan lei: Sancun jinlian* (Tears of ladies from the inner chambers: The three-inch golden lotus). Taipei: Taibei xian wenhua chu, 1998.

Ko, Dorothy. *Teachers of the Inner Chambers: Women and Culture in Seventeenth-Century China*. Stanford: Stanford University Press, 1994.

Kuhn, Dieter. *Die Darstellung des Handwebstuhls in China* (The handloom in Chinese agricultural literature before the nineteenth century). Cologne: Lindauer Dornier, 1975.

———. *Die Song-Dynastie: Eine neue Gesellschaft im Spiegel ihrer Kultur*. Weinheim: Acta Humaniora, VCH, 1987.

———. *Textile Technology: Spinning and Reeling*. Vol. 5, pt. 9 of *Science and Civilisation in China*, edited by Joseph Needham. Cambridge: Cambridge University Press, 1988.

———. *A Place for the Dead: An Archaeological Documentary on Graves and Tombs of the Song Dynasty (960–1279)*. Heidelberg: Edition Forum, 1996.

Lai, Violet L. *He Was a Ram: Wong Aloiau of Hawaii*. Honolulu: Hawaii Chinese History Center and the Wong Aloiau Association; University of Hawaii Press, 1985.

Ledderose, Lothar. *Ten Thousand Things: Module and Mass Production in Chinese Art*. A. W. Mellon Lectures in the Fine Arts 46. Princeton, N.J.: Princeton University Press, 2000.

Levy, Howard S. *Chinese Footbinding: The History of a Curious Erotic Custom*. Taipei: Southern Materials Center, 1984.

Mann, Susan. *Precious Records: Women in China's Long Eighteenth Century*. Stanford: Stanford University Press, 1997.

Mingyuan shigui cao (Poetic retrospective of famous ladies). Handwritten manuscript in the Tōyō Bunko, Tokyo, Japan. N.p., n.d.

National Palace Museum, ed. *Glimpses into the Hidden Quarters: Paintings of Women from the Middle Kingdom*. Taipei: National Palace Museum, 1998.

Ouyang, Yuqian, ed. *Tangdai wudao* (Dance cultures of the Tang dynasty). Taipei: Lanting, 1985.

Pomeranz, Kenneth. *The Great Divergence: China, Europe, and the Making of the Modern World Economy*. Princeton: Princeton University Press, 2000.

Quan Tang shi (Complete Tang poetry). Shanghai: Shanghai guji, 1995.

Quzhoushi wenguan hui. "Zhejiang Quzhoushi Nan-Song mu chutu qiwu" (Artifacts unearthed from the Southern Song tomb in Quzhou city, Zhejiang province). *Kaogu* 11 (1983): 1004–11, 1018.

Roberts, Glenn and Valerie Steele. "The Three-Inch Golden Lotus: A Collection of Chinese Bound Foot Shoes." *Arts of Asia* 27, no. 2 (1997): 69–85.

Rosen, Ruth. "Draw the Line at the Knife." *Los Angeles Times*, 17 November 1991.

Rossi, William A. *The Sex Life of the Foot and Shoe*. New York: Ballantine Books, 1978.

Ruitenbeek, Klaas. *Carpentry and Building in Late Imperial China*. Leiden: E. J. Brill, 1993.

Schafer, Edward. *The Divine Woman: Dragon Ladies and Rain Maidens*. San Francisco: North Point Press, 1980.

Shen, Shou. *Xueyi xiu pu* (Xueyi's [Shen Shou's] way of embroidery). N.p., n.d.

Steele, Valerie. *Fetish: Fashion, Sex, and Power*. New Haven: Yale University Press, 1996.

Szeto, Naomi Yin-yin. *Of Hearts and Hands: Hong Kong's Traditional Trades and Crafts*. Hong Kong: The Urban Council, 1996.

Tao, Zongyi. *Chuogeng lu* (Resting the plough). In *Siku quanshu*, Zi bu 12, Xiaoshuojia lei 1.

Thomson, John. *Illustrations of China and Its People*. London: Sampson Low, Marston, Low and Searle, 1874.

Van Gulik, R. H. *Erotic Colour Prints of the Ming Period*. Tokyo: Privately published, 1951.

Wang, Ping. *Aching for Beauty: Footbinding in China*. Minneapolis: University of Minnesota Press, 2000.

Wang, Yan. *Wanli dihou de yichu* (The wardrobes of the Ming Emperor and Empress Wanli). Taipei: Dongda, 1995.

Xu, Zhi. *Jiexiao ji* (Deeds of integrity and filial piety). In *Siku quanshu*, Ji bu 3, Bieji lei 2.

Yin, Yazhao. *Zhongguo gudian yu minwu yanjiu* (A study of classical and folk dance in China). Taipei: Guanya, 1991.

Yü, Chün-fang. "Guanyin: The Chinese Transformation of Avalokiteśvara. In *Latter Days of the Law: Images of Chinese Buddhism, 850–1850*, edited by Marsha Weidner, 150–81. Lawrence, Ks.: Spencer Museum of Art, University of Kansas; Honolulu: University of Hawaii Press, 1994.

———. *Kuan-yin: The Chinese Transformation of Avalokiteśvara*. New York: Columbia University Press, 2001.

Yuan, He. *Zhongguo wudao yixiang lun* (A study of the concepts and aesthetics of Chinese dance). Beijing: Wenhua yishu, 1994.

Zabaojang jing (The Sutra on the Storehouse of Sundry Valuables). Vol. 4 of *Taishō shinshū daizōkyō* (The Tripitaka in Chinese), edited by Takakusu Junjirō and Watanabe Kaigyoku. Tokyo: Taishō Issaikyō kankōkai, 1924–34.

Zhang, Bangji. *Mozhuang manlu* (Random notes from the Ink Estate). In *Siku quanshu*, Zi bu 10, Zajia lei 3.

Zhou, Wu. *Zhongguo banhua shi tulu* (A pictorial history of Chinese woodblock prints). Shanghai: Renmin meishu, 1988.

Zhu, Qixin. "Royal Costumes of the Jin Dynasty." *Orientations* (December 1990). Reprinted in *Chinese and Central Asian Textiles: Selected Articles from Orientations, 1983–1997*. Hong Kong: Orientations Magazine, 1998.

PHOTOGRAPHY CREDITS

Numbers refer to figures unless otherwise indicated.

Photographs by Hal Roth: Frontis., 1, 8, 9, 15, 21, 22, 33, 35, 38, 48, 49, 52, 54, 60, 73, 74, 77, 78, 82, 83, p. 27, p. 156

Photographs by Ron Wood: 2, 3, 4, 5, 20, 23, 24, 27, 28, 30, 31, 32, 34, 37, 42, 43, 50, 51, 53, 56, 57, 58, 61, 62, 64, 65, 66, 68, 69, 70, 71, 75, 76, 80, 84

Permission to reprint images from publications:
    Bibliothèque Nationale de France: 36
    Cambridge University Press: p. 78
    Dennis George Crow: 47
    Dingling Museum: 13
    Fujian Province Museum: 10, 19 (below)
    Heilongjiang Province Cultural and Archeological Relics Institute: 12
    Chi-sheng Ko, *Shengui hongyan lei*: 26, 39
    Princeton University Press: three diagrams on pp. 56–57
    Shanghai Literature and Art Publishing House: 11
    National Palace Museum, Taipei, Taiwan, Republic of China: 14

Permission to reprint from original photographs in their collections:
    Douglas D. L. Chong: 85, 86, 87
    Dr. Chi-sheng Ko: 45, 46, 81, p. 4

Permission for artifacts in their collections to be photographed for this book:
    Douglas D. L. Chong: 2, 5, 34, 43, 76, 88, 89
    Vincent V. Comer: 28, 42, 51, 53, 56, 58, p. 5
    Hawaii Plantation Village: 76
    Dr. Chi-sheng Ko: 2, 2, 3, 3, 3, 4, 23, 23, 23, 24, 24, 24, 27, 27, 32, 34, 34, 37, 37, 39, 42, 42, 42, 42, 43, 56, 61, 62, 66, 68, 69, 70, 80 (repeated numbers indicate multiple shoes in group photographs)
    Ruth Chandler Williamson Gallery, Scripps College: 4

INDEX

Amiot, Père, *80*

Among the Flowers, 34–35, 45

Amoy, 132

Anhui style, *120*, 121, *121*

animal shoes, 77; pig, *49*; tiger, *47*

anklets, embroidered, *90*; fashion trends in, 93–94

anti-footbinding movement, 15, 133, 148n5

antique collecting, 143

appliqué, *8*, *11*, 85, 91, *112*

arched shoes (*gongxie*), 17

architecture, imaginary, 56, 57

Astana, Tang-dynasty tomb at, *39*, *43*

auspicious days, for first binding, 63–64

bamboo motif, 25

bat motif, 104, 107, *126*, *129*

Bata, Sonja, 12

Bata Princess shoes, *140*, 141

Bata Shoe Museum, 12, 17

binding cloth, 42, 54, 55, 98, 99, 132

Book of Rites, 56

booties, 72, 99, 111, 112; Jin style, with curled toes, *115*; Shandong-style, in red and black silk, decorated with lotus and goldfish, *106*; Shandong-style, in stiff dark blue and gray satin with cuff, *113*; Shandong-style varnished, *14*; Shandong-style wedding, in red satin with decorated sole, *71*; Shanxi-style, of embroidered red silk and black cotton, *101*; Shanxi-style mourning, *74*. *See also* boots

boots, 99, 124; Cantonese, of turquoise and hot pink satin with split heels, *129*; northern-style, with inner heel, *102*; Shanxi, 124. *See also* booties; overshoes

boudoir poetry, 31, 34

Bound Foot of a Chinese Lady (photo), *130*

Bray, Francesca, 57

bride price, 50

Broken Battle Formation dances, 37

Buddhism, 66, 150n3 (chap. 2). *See also* Guanyin

butterfly motif, *112*, 124, *137*

Cantonese opera, 62

Cantonese shoes, 124–25, 127–28, 141; boots of turquoise and hot pink satin with split heels, *129*; components of, *146*; made in Hawaii, *144*; in pale yellow silk with slightly curved wedge heels, *126*; patterns for, *145*; shoe-making, 91

Cao Zijian, "Rhapsody on the Luo River Goddess" by, 30, *30*, 149n4

carp, 25, 26, 28

Cave of Tidal Waves, 66

Centennial Exhibition of 1876 (Philadelphia), 151n3

chicken motif, 124

childbirth, 54, 80

children's shoes, 77; pig, *49*; tiger, *47*

Chinese family, 49, 50–52

Chinese house, 56–57

Ching Hung Yau, *142*

Ching Kan You, 141, *142*, 143, *144*

Ching family of Honolulu: homestead, *143*; photograph of, *142*; shoe patterns used by, *145*, *146*

Chong, Douglas D. L., 128, 141; grandmother of, *142*

Chun Mun Chu (Mrs.), *142*

Cinderella story, 25, 41, 44

clay figurines, of stylish ladies in cloud-tip shoes, *40*

clogs, varnished, *14*

cloud-tip shoes, *43*; male, from Astana tomb, *39*; on painted clay figurines of stylish ladies, *40*; slippers, 39–40

coin motif, 104, *105*, 109

commercial economy, 111, 121, 134, 150n2 (chap. *3*)

Confucianism, 15, 45, 51, 56, 79; court ceremonies, 36–37

cotton, 80–81, 116

courtyard house, 56, *57*

crescent-shaped feet, 42, *43*, 44

curled toes, 114, *115*

Dabei Dharani of the Bodhisattva Guanyin in Thirty-Two Manifestations, 67

dance: ballet, 10; Central Asian influence in, 37–38, 41, 44; in Confucian court ceremonies, 36–37; Dragon Pond, 38–39; lion, 37; military, 37, 38; and origins of footbinding, 35; Rainbow Skirt and Feathered Cape, 39–40, 43; sensuality in, 37; small footsteps in, 40–41; Tazhi, 38, 40, 42, 149n7

Daoist goddesses, *36*, 72

Daoist immortals, 28, 107–109

Daoshan xinwen, 149n11

Datong style, 114, 127; high-heeled shoes with fine lacing, *114*

daughters: in the Chinese family, 28, 49, 50; mothers and, 61, 85–87; peasant, 12, 61; in the Yexian story, 26–27, 28

De'an (Jiangxi province), tomb at, 24, 149n3

design motifs, 104–5, 109; favored by the Cantonese, 124; hand-painted, *14*, 85; visual puns, 107. *See also* appliqué; bat motif; butterfly motif; coin motif; embroidery; fish motif; geometric motifs; lotus; rooster motif; shoe motif; swastika motif

Ding Pei, 87–88

domesticity: and Confucianism, 45, 56–57; and cotton production, 80–81; and footbinding, 17, 18, 52

Donghun, Duke of, 32

dowry, 50

Dragon Pond dance, 38–39

Edison, Thomas, 22

Eight Immortals, 107–109

embroidered slippers (*xiuxie*), 17

embroidery: on anklets and leggings, *90*; as art, 85, 88; and commercial components, 121; designs on shoe uppers, 83, 85, *86*, 88, *89*, *91*; and domestic culture, 18, 85–89; examination candidate on horseback, *68*; on gift shoes, 75; on Huizhou shoes, 121; on imperial footwear, 25; on Jiang-Zhe shoes, 127; on Jin-style shoes, 114; on "minority shoes," 118; multicolor with gold metal thread, 27; prayer on votive shoes, 65; and reaction to footbinding, 10; on Shandong-style booties, *106*; in shoe-making process, 81; on shoes from Anhui, *120*, 121, *121*; on shoes from Ningbo and Shaoxing, 122; on soles of funerary shoes, *73*; on Taiwan-style shoes, *117*; on training shoes, 62; on wedding shoes, 52. *See also* design motifs

embroidery frame, 82, 87

embroidery manuals, 87–88, *87*

erotic art, 10, 92–93, *93*

eroticism of feet and shoes, 18, 19, 34–35

ethnic minorities, 118

Every Step a Lotus (exhibition), 12

examination candidates, *68*

exhibitions, 12, 147, 151n3

Fan Hong, 148n5

father-son tie, 61

female kinship, 61–63

Feng Jicai, 148n5

fengshui (geomancy), 56

Fernsebner, Susan R., 151n3

fertility, 75; association with the foot, 25, 35; and sericulture, 79–80; symbols, 25, 67, 107

fish: carp, 25, 26, 28; as fertility symbol, 25

fish motif, 104, *106*, 107, *117*

foot: association with fertility, 25, 35; bones of, 60; and sexuality, 19, 25, 34–35

footbinding: condemnation of, 10, 44–45, 148n2; and cotton technology, 81; decline of, 19, 133, 140; domestication of, 17, 45, 52; and ethnic background, 12, 15; and female identity, 17, 19, 97; and female sensuality, 44; first, 54, 58, 61, 63–64, 69, 150n1 (chap. 2); fixation on size and measurement, 25, 32; gait associated with, 60, 104; image of, 9–10; loose, 138; in lower-class and peasant households, 12, 52, 61, 80–81, 112; and marriage prospects, 52, 61; materials needed for, 54, 55, 58; as a meaningful practice, 147; missionary accounts of, 12, 133; and national shame, 147,

151n3; origins of, 21–22, 32, 42, 44–45; pain of, 15, 54, 104; photography and, 131–32; physical effects of, 60, 98–99, 104; professional, 141; and social status, 81; in the Southern Song, 24; steps in, 59; and the value of girls, 28; Tang-dynasty evidence for, 31–32, 34, 35; and textile work, 52–54; textual record of, 18; in the twentieth century, 133–38

foot fetishists, 10, 15
foot powder, 54–58, 55
footwear: evolution of, 43; imperial, from Jin kingdom, 24; imperial, from tomb of Ming emperor Wanli, 25; outdoor, 10. See also shoes
Fragrant Toilette genre, 31, 35
French knot stitches, 120, 121
Fujian province, 21, 58, 116. See also Huang Sheng, tomb of
funerary objects, shoes as, 23–24
funerary shoes, 75; blue cotton, with black cotton band and embroidered soles, 73

Gates, Hill, 150n2 (chap. 3)
geometric motifs, 119, 128
gift shoes, 69, 72, 75, 139; stitched for presentation on tasseled green silk, 70
gilded lilies (jinlian), 17
Goddess of the River Luo, 30, 30, 38
gongxie (arched shoes), 17
good-luck symbols, 104–5, 107
Guangdong province, 124; shoe-making in, 91. See also Cantonese shoes
Guanyin, 66–67, 67, 75, 150n3 (chap. 2)

Hakka, 12–15
Han Chinese, 12
Han dynasty, 12
Han Wo, 45; poem "Ode to the Slippers" by, 31–34
Hawaii: Cantonese immigrants to, 125, 128, 141, 144; Cantonese shoes in, 144, 145, 146; Ching family homestead, 143; footbinding in, 128, 142
He Xiangu, 107–109
heels: on Cantonese shoes, 124–25; cylindrical, on Ming imperial footwear, 25; cylindrical, with back flap of pale blue cotton, 13; double, 125; drum-shaped, 114; gathered, 116; guava-wood, 144; high, 103, 103, 114; high wedge, in Fujian and Taiwan shoes, 116; inner, 101–103, 102; kidney-shaped, 112; Shandong-style decorated, 112; of southern shoes, 122; southern split, 125, 129; tabs on, 33, 34, 92, 117; wooden, 83, 91
heel straps, 124
high-heeled shoes, 103, 103; Datong-style, with fine lacing, 114. See also Taiwan style
Hong Kong Heritage Museum, 150n3 (chap. 3)
Horsehead Lady, 78, 79
Houyi, 28
Huang Sheng: shoes of, 21, 21, 22, 23, 43; tomb of, 21, 149n1
Huizhou merchants, 121
Huizhou shoes, 121, 127

imperial footwear, 24, 25
inner heels, 101–103, 102

interior northwest and southwest shoes, 118, 118, 119

Jade Ring Yang. See Yang Guifei
Jiangsu/Zhejiang region, 69, 122, 127; dark blue satin low-heeled pumps, 123; ladder-rung shoes, 123; pale blue silk shoes with damask insert, 122
jianzui xie (pointy tip shoes), 134–35
jiaodai. See leg sashes
Jin kingdom, imperial footwear from, 24
jinlian (gilded lilies), 17
Jin style, 114; booties with curled toes, 115
Jurchens, 24

kang (platform bed), 111
Kannon, 150n3 (chap. 2). See also Guanyin
Kitchen God, 64

ladder-rung shoes (wangzi xie), 122, 127; in pale blue silk embroidered with gold thread, 123
Lan Caihe, 109
Lanxi (Zhejiang province), 149n3
leather, 134, 135
leggings (oufu; xiku), 92–93; ankletlike, in Ming erotic print, 93; fashion trends and regional differences, 93–94, 94, 95; long, in red silk with blue trim, 90; northern woman with pants gathered inside, 94
leg sashes (jiaodai), 93, 94; women weaving, with hand loom, 80
Lei Zu (Empress Xiling), 78, 79
Levy, Howard, Chinese Footbinding by, 18
Li Yü, 42
Liu Hai, 109

longevity shoes, 75; blue cotton, with black cotton band and embroidered soles, 73

lotus: associated with bound feet, 32, 44; in Dragon Pond dance, 38–39; and Guanyin cult, 66–67, 67; motif, 25, 106, 108, 117, 124, 137; on soles of funerary shoes, 73, 75; in story of Yaoniang, 42; as visual pun, 46, 107

lotus shoes: collections of, 17, 143–44; and foot size, 98–99, 101, 102; new-style, 134–35, 135, 136, 139; regional styles, 99, 109–11, 121; as souvenirs, 141; use of term, 17. See also shoes

Lotus Sutra, 66

Luke See Chin (Mrs.), 142

luo (silk tabby), 21, 22

Luo Shuangshuang, 23, 23

Ma, Madame, poem by, 72

Malacca, 62, 141

Malaya, 141

Manchus, 12, 140; Jurchen ancestors of, 24

Mann, Susan, 150n2 (chap. 3)

Marcos, Imelda, 144

marriage, 52, 61–63. See also wedding shoes

Mawei, 39, 41

Ming emperor Wanli, tomb of, 25

"minority shoes," 118

missionaries, 12, 133, 143

Moon Goddess, 34

mother-daughter tie, 61

motherhood, 79–80

mothers-in-law, 75; gift shoes for, 69

mourning shoes, 75; northern-style, with white tuft on tip, 75; Shanxi-style, in pale yellow with purple tuft, 74; Shanxi-style booties, 74

museums, 144

musical instruments, 36

nationalism, 140, 147, 151n3

natural foot movement, 133

needlework pattern books, 86

Ningbo, 122, 127

Northern Song dynasty, 41

northern-style shoes: booties with ornate soles, 111; in lilac pink silk with blue silk vamp appliqué, 8; outdoor, 91; in red silk with gently arched wooden sole, 20. See also Shandong style; Shanxi style

opium implements, 151n3

origins of cultural phenomena, 22–23. See also footbinding, origins of oufu. See leggings

overseas Chinese, 140–41

overshoes: padded overboots, 16; soft-sided, 13; southern-style, 11

Pan, Consort, 32, 34

party shoes, 125

peach blossom motif, 124

Philippines, 141

photography, 131–32; Bound Foot of a Chinese Lady, 130, 132; Seated Woman Showing One Unwrapped Bound Foot, 96, 98; of the shoe-making process, 150n3 (chap. 3)

pig shoes, 49

pine motif, 25

platform bed (kang), 111

pleasure quarters, 41–42

plum-blossom motif, 21

poetry, 28, 30–34; boudoir, 31, 34; song-lyrics, 34–35

poets. See Cao Zijian; Han Wo; Ma, Madame; Shen Yixiu

pointy tip shoes (jianzui xie), 134–35; embroidered, in red silk with leather sole, 137

pumps: low-heel, 127; Shaoxing-style, in dark blue satin, 100

qiao xie (stilt shoes), 62

Qing dynasty, 12

Qinghai, embroidered shoes with geometric patterns and upturned toes from, 119

Queen Mother of the West, 72

Quzhou (Zhejiang province), tomb at, 23

Rainbow Skirt and Feathered Cape dance, 39–40, 43

rain shoes, with hand-painted designs, 14, 85

regional styles, 110, 111, 121, 127–28. See also Anhui style; Cantonese shoes; Datong style; interior northwest and southwest shoes; Jiangsu/Zhejiang region; northern-style shoes; Shandong style; Shanxi style; southern-style shoes; Taiwan style

rice balls, 64

riding boots, 38, 41

Roman key motif, 113

rooster motif, 108

Ruitenbeek, Klaas, 57

St. Louis Exposition, 147

sandals, straw, 16

sericulture, 78, 79–80, 127

Seven Heavenly Maidens, *125*

sewing, 69, 72; sewing machine, *19*; sewing scissors, *55*. *See also* embroidery; shoe-making

Shandong, 150n3 (chap. 3)

Shandong style, 111, 112; booties, 112; booties in red and black silk, decorated with lotus and goldfish, *106*; decorated soles, *112*; heel with embroidered butterfly, *112*; shoes in pink silk with arched wooden sole, *113*; stiff dark blue and gray satin booties with cuff, *113*; wedding bootie, *71*

Shanghai, 138

Shanxi style, 111, 114; booties of embroidered red silk and black cotton, *101*; boots, 124; Datong-style high-heeled shoes, *114*; Jin-style booties with curled toes, *115*; mourning shoes, *74*; shoes with curled toes in red satin with embroidered vamp, *115*

Shaoxing, 122, 127; style pumps in dark blue satin, *100*

Shen Shou, 88

Shen Yixiu, 85–87

Shi Shengzu, tomb of, 23, *23*

shoe components, Cantonese, *146*

shoe laces, 92, 93, 99, *103*, 114, 135

shoe-making: Cantonese shoes, 124–25; in Chinese villages today, 77; decoration of uppers, 83–85; in domestic life, 18, *18*, 69, 77; finishing, 92; in Hunan, 77; interviews on and photos of, 150n3 (chap. 3); modern sewing machine used in, *19*; outdoor shoes, 91, 92; preparation of uppers, 91–92; professional, 138; regional styles, 111, 128; soft-soled sleeping slippers, 83; technique for, 81; tools for, 82, 83. *See also* shoe-pattern books

shoe motif, 105, *105*, 107

shoe-pattern books, 83, 86; woodblock print of domestic women using, *18*; woodblock print showing shoe-making with modern sewing machine, *19*

shoe patterns, *145*. *See also* shoe-pattern books

shoes: animal, 47, 49, 77; black leather Oxford with cotton laces, *135*; black patent leather, with instep strap and leather sole, *135*; black satin, with turquoise embroidery and double cross-over straps, *139*; blue homemade, with fabric upper and all-cotton heels, *84*; brocade, for the Southeast Asian market, *140*; with brown silk *luo*-tabby upper from tomb of Lady Huang Sheng, *21*; children's, 47, 49, 77; crescent-shaped, *43*; dark blue satin, with embroidered motif of successful examination candidate, *68*; elongated, from Suzhou, *64*; with embroidered rooster, lotus, and swastika, *108*; embroidered, with green band, white insert, and heel tab lined in red, *33*; for first binding, 58, 69; green *luo*-gauze, of queen of Jin, *24*; as items of fashion, 104, 134; kung-fu, 77; leather, with elastic gusset and stacked leather heel, *135*; left and right pairings of, 91, *135*; outdoor, 72, 83, 91; pale red silk, with upturned toe, from tomb of Ming emperor Wanli, *25*; with pink silk vamp and ribbon cuff, *76*; in pink silk with arched wedge heel covered in blue silk, *20*; from Qinghai with upturned toe and geometric patterns, *119*; in red cotton with layered cotton sole from interior region, *119*; red silk, with embroidered shoe motif, *105*; red silk, with overhanging toes from Sichuan province, *118*; silver, with dramatic upturned toe, from the tomb of Shi Shengzu, 23, *23*; Tang-dynasty male, made of hemp, *43*; tips of, emerging from wide-legged pants with trim, *95*; with upturned toes, 21, 22, 23–24, 25, 30, *119*; to wear in the bedroom, 72. *See also* booties; Cantonese shoes; clogs; cloud-tip shoes; footwear; funerary shoes; gift shoes; high-heeled shoes; ladder-rung shoes; lotus shoes; mourning shoes; northern-style shoes; overshoes; pointy tip shoes; rain shoes; sandals; Shandong style; Shanxi style; shoe-making; sleeping shoes; slippers; snow shoes; southern-style shoes; Taiwan style; toad shoes; training shoes; votive shoes; wedding shoes

shoe uppers: decoration of, 83–85; partially finished, *89*; predecorated, 88, *89*; preparation of, 91–92

Sichuan province, red silk shoes with overhanging toes from, *118*

silk, 79–80. *See also* sericulture

Silk Road, 79

silk tabby (*luo*), 21, 22

silkworm goddesses, 78

silkworm maiden, legend of, 78, 79

Singapore, 141; training shoes from, *62*

sleeping shoes, *13*, 69–72, *111*; red cotton, with quilted sole and heel area, *71*; socklike, with curled toe in blue cotton, *13*

slippers: cloud-tip, with upturned toe, 39–40; dancing, *38*; eroticism of, 35; golden, in Yexian story, 25, 26–27; silk "distant roaming," worn by Goddess of the River Luo, 30–31, *30*; sleeping, making of, 83; tiny silk, embroidered in multicolor silk floss and gold metal thread, *27*; worn under booties, *111*

snow shoes, felt with layered fabric sole, *16*

soles: decorated, *2*, *112*; northern-style arched wooden, *89*; soft, 83; of southern shoes, 122; wooden, 83, 85, 91

Song dynasty: dance, 149n7; marriage in, 52. *See also* Northern Song dynasty; Southern Song dynasty

song-lyrics, 34–35

sons, 61, 75

Southeast Asia, 140, *140*

Southern Song dynasty: China under, 29; footbinding in, 24; shoe styles of, 23; tombs, 24, 149n3. *See also* Huang Sheng; Shi Shengzu, tomb of southern-style shoes: dark blue satin low-heeled pumps with shallow vamp, *123*; pale blue silk, with white damask insert, *122*; in red silk, expressing wish for many children, *46*; structure of, 127

Southern Tang kingdom, 42–43

Southland, 28, 34, 43

souvenirs, 141

statecraft philosophy, 80

stilt shoes (*qiao xie*), 62

Stove God, 64

Suzhou, 64, 127

swastika motif, 107, *108*

Tadzhikistan, 38

Taiwan, 58, 111, 147. *See also* Taiwan style

Taiwan style, 111, 116; embroidered shoes with brown upper and orange heel area, *117*; shoes in dark blue cotton with gathered heel, *116*; shoes in red silk with turquoise silk back, *103*; wedding shoes, 53

Tang dynasty: dance, 35–41; figurines of stylish ladies, *40*; influences from South and Central Asia, 37, 41; marriage in, 52

Tang emperor Xuanzong, 39

Tao Zongyi, 149n11

Tazhi dance, 38, 40, 42, 149n7

textiles, 18, 34, 52, 79, 150n2 (chap. 3). *See also* cotton; shoe-making; silk

Thomson, John, 131–32; *Illustrations of China and Its People* by, *130*, 131

tiger shoes, 47

Tiny-Footed Maiden, 64–66

toad motif, 109

toad shoes, 58; with bare wooden heel used in the second stage of training, 62; flat, in quilted and embroidered cotton, 62

Tom Chung (Mrs.), *142*

Tom You (Mrs.), *142*

tombs: at Astana, 39, 43; of Huang Sheng, 21–23, *21*, *43*, 149n3 (chap. 1); of Madame Zhou, 24; of Ming emperor Wanli, 25; of Shi Shengzu, 23, *23*

training shoes, 58; red, with painted wooden heels, from Singapore, *62*. *See also* toad shoes

trousseau, 69, 70, *139*

Tsui, Madam Mei-wah, 150n3 (chap. 3)

Tuohan, king of, 26, 27

turtle motif, *117*

"Vegetarian," 138

visual puns, 46, 107

votive shoes, 66, 69; Cantonese, 125, *125*; with embroidered prayer, *65*

Wang Ping, 148n5

wangzi xie (ladder-rung shoes), 122, *122*, 127

Water and Moon Guanyin, 67

Way of Embroidery (Xiu pu), 88

weaving, *80*

Weaving Maid, 34; and the Cowherd, *125*

wedding shoes, 69–72, *71*; northern-style, in red silk with gold leaf decoration on sole, 52; Shandong-style bootie in red satin with decorated sole, *71*; southern-style, in red silk and decorated with golden and silver couching, 52; Taiwan-style, in embroidered red satin, 52; Taiwan-style, in plain red satin, 52

Wei Jiuding, scroll of Goddess of the River Luo by, *30*

Wen Tingyun, "Rhapsody of the Brocade Shoe," 34

Western influence, 135, *135*, *136*

White-Robed Guanyin, 67, *67*

womanly work (*nügong*), 17, 52, 79–80, 138

women: mothers-in-law, 69, 75; old, 75; role in Chinese household, 56–57, 61–63; verse and prose written by, 18, 69, 72

woodblock prints: of domestic women making shoes, *18*; and shoe patterns, *83*; showing women working with modern sewing machine, *19*
Wu Zongyuan, scroll *Procession of Immortals Paying Homage to the Primordial*, *36*
Wu-the-Cave, 26, 27

Xiamen, 132
Xiao Baojian, 32
Xicun village (Zhongshan county), *144*
xiku. See leggings
Xiling, Empress, 78, 79
Xiu pu (Way of embroidery), 88
xiuxie (embroidered slippers), 17
Xu Zhi, 45

Yang Guifei, 39, 40–41
Yaoniang, 42–43, 149n11
Yellow Emperor, 58, 79
Yellow Emperor's Classic of Internal Medicine, 58
Yeo Sing Guat, 141
Yexian, 25, 26–27, 28, 30
Yi county (Huizhou prefecture, Anhui province), 121
Yongzhou (Guangxi province), 28
Yuan dynasty, scroll of Goddess of the River Luo, *30*
Yuen Sock (Mrs.), *142*
Yuen Yun Kong (Mrs.), *125*
Yunnan, footbinding in, 133

Zhang Bangji, *Mozhuang manlu* by, 149n6
Zhejiang. *See* Jiangsu/Zhejiang region
Zhongshan (Guangdong province), *125*, 141, *144*
Zhou, Madame, tomb of, 24, 149n3
Zhou Mi, 149n11
Zhou, Southern Tang senior queen, 43
zodiac animals, 47, 48

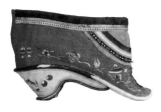

Every Step a Lotus

Produced by Joseph N. Newland, Q.E.D.
Design and composition by Sandy Bell
Manuscript edited by Patricia Draher Kiyono
Editorial assistance by Olga Sledziewski
Proofread by Sharon Rose Vonasch
Index by Susan Stone
Cartography by David Fuller, DLF Group

Printed by Friesens, Manitoba, Canada

Titling set in Serlio.
Text set in Granjon and Bernhard Gothic.